Louise Callan, RSCJ

(1893-1966): HISTORIAN AND BIOGRAPHER
OF PHILIPPINE DUCHESNE

Louise Callan, RSCJ

(1893-1966): HISTORIAN AND BIOGRAPHER OF PHILIPPINE DUCHESNE

Carolyn Osiek, RSCJ

Louise Callan, RSCJ (1893-1966):
Historian and Biographer of Philippine Duchesne

iUniverse books may be ordered through booksellers or by contacting:

iUniverse
1663 Liberty Drive
Bloomington, IN 47403
www.iuniverse.com
1-800-Authors (1-800-288-4677)

Because of the dynamic nature of the Internet, any web addresses or links contained in this book may have changed since publication and may no longer be valid. The views expressed in this work are solely those of the author and do not necessarily reflect the views of the publisher, and the publisher hereby disclaims any responsibility for them.

Any people depicted in stock imagery provided by Thinkstock are models, and such images are being used for illustrative purposes only.
Certain stock imagery © Thinkstock.

ISBN: 978-1-4917-7498-4 (sc)
ISBN: 978-1-4917-7499-1 (e)

Print information available on the last page.

iUniverse rev. date: 08/19/2015

CONTENTS

Introduction vii

Early Years 1

Into the Society of the Sacred Heart 4

Mother Callan, Author and College Professor 11

Memories of Students and Community 16

The Lectures on Mother Duchesne 22

The View through Relationship 26

The Biograhy Appears and Sets a Future Course 34

To the New Maryville Campus 46

Unexpectedly, the End 72

Acknowledgements 81

INTRODUCTION

One might well ask: why remember Louise Callan, RSCJ, nearly fifty years after her death? During her lifetime she was a dearly loved college teacher, a loyal friend, a superb scholar, and a well-respected historian and biographer. She was the author of two books of crucial importance for the Society of the Sacred Heart: *The Society of the Sacred Heart in North America* (1937) and *Philippine Duchesne: Pioneer Missionary of the Sacred Heart* (1957). Both books had still wider importance and were received with extensive critical acclaim among scholars of American Catholic history.

After the beatification of Blessed Philippine in 1940, the Archdiocese of Saint Louis saw the need for a suitable shrine to her in Saint Charles and began plans for the building that was completed in 1952. At the same time, Louise Callan saw the need for another kind of tribute to the new *beata*: a critical biography that would take into account the American context and a more contemporary understanding of Philippine Duchesne in her own times. Mother Callan knew Philippine Duchesne as no one beyond Philippine's contemporaries did. The depth of her research and insight into the saint have yet to be surpassed after half a century and Philippine's canonization by the Church in 1988.

As we prepare for the bicentennial of the arrival of Saint Rose Philippine Duchesne to America in 1818 and the launch of international mission in the Society of the Sacred Heart, remembering Louise Callan and the part she played half a century ago is a fitting part of our preparation for remembering the events of two hundred years ago.

Some might view it simply as a gentle irony: a noted historian's life left untold, despite her painstaking research to tell the story of others. Just before Louise Callan, RSCJ, distinguished historian of the *Society of the Sacred Heart in North America*, official biographer of Saint Rose Philippine Duchesne, and researcher revered among her contemporaries as an expert on pioneer life, died—the international Society of the Sacred Heart ceased publication of its *Annual Letters*, an intra-Society publication that included memorials of the lives of religious who die each year. The account of Louise's life and death therefore reached only the circle of those who knew her directly. It seems fitting finally to celebrate the historian, dedicated teacher, and unusually gifted woman who was in our midst. The origin of this project rests on a small batch of letters that Louise wrote to her former student and dear friend Margaret Byrne, Religious of the Cenacle, which Margaret made available some years ago. Covering a period of fifteen years between 1952 and 1966, the year of Louise's death, they document much of her life during those years, her joys, struggles, and heroic endurance of suffering from the cancer that would eventually take her life. In combination with testimonies of others who knew her and evidence of her scholarly achievement, they are the base upon which this biography is built.

EARLY YEARS

Not much can be known about Louise's childhood. Other than the basic facts, the three sources are an article written by Louise herself in *The Maryville Magazine* (vol. 33, May, 1958), an article written by her friend Marion Bascom, RSCJ[1] in the same publication in 1967 after Louise's death, and the memories of Margaret Byrne, RC. Louise's article, "Mother Shaw: As I Knew Her," is an account of Louise's first encounter with Mother Cora Shaw, RSCJ, at her arrival for boarding school at the Convent of the Sacred Heart, Clifton, Cincinnati, for the second year of high school. The focus is on Mother Shaw, who had recently died at Maryville College. Marion Bascom's information must have come directly from Louise, since they lived long years together at Maryville.

Anne Louise Callan was born in Knoxville, Tennessee, on December 8, 1893, Feast of the Immaculate Conception, for which reason her mother wanted to name her Immaculata, but her father refused! She was the youngest of ten children of Frank J. Callan and Sarah Riley Callan, with a big age gap between her and her next oldest sibling. Three of the children died in childhood, one of them before she was born. Louise was baptized on December 24 of the same year. Marion Bascom notes that all of Louise's older siblings took a hand in raising her, which may account for her lively personality that always had a quick retort to offer. Even as a child, she was gifted musically and could improvise on the piano so well that her brothers would take her to the silent movies and have her play at the theatre the piano accompaniment that was expected to complement the action of the film.

[1] Marion Bascom, RSCJ, was born in Saint Louis in 1903. She entered the Society in 1926 and was professed in 1934. After teaching at Clifton, Villa Duchesne, and City House in Saint Louis, she earned an advanced degree at Oxford after profession and was from 1937-1971 Professor of English at Maryville. She died at Oakwood in 2000.

Louise's later comments about her semi-invalid mother were none too complimentary: "Whenever mama didn't want to face something she had a heart attack." But she held her father in great esteem and reverence. She enjoyed walks with him on Sundays, when he told her to avoid puddles and walk with good posture. With her musical talent, she could attend a concert of popular songs and play them by ear.

There was a military influence in the family: her brother Robert Emmet (1874-1936) attended West Point as a classmate of General Douglas MacArthur, was a veteran of the Spanish-American War and World War I, and would himself become a five-star general. Camp Callan in San Diego, California, an anti-aircraft replacement training center during World War II, was named after him in 1940.[2] During World War II, when the Religious of the Sacred Heart were in difficulties in Japan, Louise wrote to General MacArthur on the basis of her deceased brother's military status, asking him to intervene, which he did.

Where Louise attended elementary school is unknown. She made her First Communion on May 27, 1906. Her college transcript indicates that she began secondary education at Knoxville High School. Several of her sisters had attended high school at Convent of the Sacred Heart, Clifton, Cincinnati, and Louise eventually followed. She went to Clifton for three years, 1910-1913. She did not want to go there. Her mother did not want her to go there. But go she did, accompanied by her father, who upon leaving said to Mother Cora Shaw,[3] the mistress general: "I leave this child in your hands." Louise's account, which may have been somewhat enhanced, was that she was indeed a handful. For weeks she hated the school, the nuns, and everything else. She cried her way through everything, hoping that they would send her home. But Mother Shaw told her: "You are not homesick, you are just boysick."

---

[2] Camp Callan closed in 1945 and the land was sold off in small parcels. www.militarymuseum.org/CpCallan.html, accessed July 2, 2012.

[3] Cora Elizabeth Shaw, RSCJ, was born in 1871 in Farmington, Missouri. She entered the Society at Maryville, making first vows in 1893. She was professed in Paris in 1899. Besides serving at Clifton, Cincinnati, she also lived and worked in Saint Michaels, Grand Coteau, New Orleans, City House in Saint Louis, and Saint Charles. She died at Maryville in 1958, with Louise in attendance at her bedside.

The Primes book for those years is extant, however[4]: she got steady *Très Biens*, week after week, so she was not the uncooperative girl that she later portrayed herself to be. She stayed, and eventually became "nunsick." She allowed herself to be deeply influenced by the religious, especially Mother Shaw, who set high standards but was also loving and understanding.

Louise emphasized two things from Mother Shaw's teaching. The first was love of the Eucharist and the importance of attendance at daily Mass, which she conveyed through General Instruction, the weekly conference that the mistress general gave to all the high school students. The second was that she taught the students how to meditate on the Gospels. After night prayers, those who wished remained behind while she led them in preparation for their prayer the next morning, in the same way that the religious were taught to do in the novitiate. When Louise confided to Mother Shaw that she thought she had a religious vocation, Mother Shaw showed no surprise. They talked about the implications, and then Mother Shaw put her hand on Louise's and said: "If you have a vocation, my dear, you cannot dream of the happiness life holds for you."

---

[4]   In Sacred Heart schools, the first activity on Monday morning was *Primes*, an assembly of the whole school and teachers at which the conduct of each student was reviewed, class by class. *Très Bien* (Very Good) was the highest level of conduct, followed by *Bien* (Good), *Assez Bien* (Good Enough), and at the bottom *Indifférent* and worst of all, "No notes."

INTO THE SOCIETY OF
THE SACRED HEART

Louise entered religious life at the age of twenty, accepted by Reverend Mother Mary Reid for the Saint Louis Vicariate. Clifton may have had at that time the six-year program that many Sacred Heart schools did then in imitation of the French system, until the growing four-year college movement in the United States made them change,[5] so she probably went from school to the novitiate within a few months. She entered the novitiate at Kenwood,[6] Albany, New York, on February 21, 1914—and left on March 25. The structured and confined way of life that characterized the novitiate was just too much for her vivacious temperament. She returned home, and one day when she was playing the piano, her mother said to her: "Louise, you know you made a mistake." She answered, "Yes, I did make a big mistake, and I'm going back." Mother Shaw had to intercede for her to return. The second time, she got as far as Kenwood, but all the horrors came back to her. She didn't cross over to the novitiate side of the house, but turned around and went home.

In those days entrance into religious life was already considered culturally as a life commitment, even though the process of formation would require several years before a decision was made. By this time, her father was so ashamed of her for leaving that he met her train at a small

---

[5] Clifton adopted the American four-year college system from 1915-1935 (Patricia Byrne, "A Tradition of Education of Women: The Society of the Sacred Heart and Higher Education," *U.S. Catholic Historian* 13.4 [1995]: 49 n. 1).

[6] The house in Albany, New York, opened its school in 1859. From the earliest years it was the novitiate for the eastern United States, and for some years for the entire United States and sometimes Canada. In 1975, the school merged with St. Agnes Episcopal School to become the Doane Stuart School, which withdrew from the property in 2008. The same year, the house was closed.

station some distance from Knoxville so that she would not be seen by his friends returning home. He would not walk down the street with her. After eight months, she realized once again that she had made a mistake, and was ready to return. Her brother Emmet by this time was an Army officer in California and wanted her to come there for a year, probably to meet some of his friends. But she refused that invitation and said she was going back to Kenwood – but this time her father would not pay for the ticket. Another brother solved the standoff by buying from her a diamond ring her father had given her so that she would have the money to buy the return ticket. He also had to take her to the train station, as her parents by this time would have nothing to do with it. She re-entered the novitiate on December 7, and this time she stayed, under the wise guidance of Mistress of Novices Mother Gertrude Bodkin.[7] She received the habit on April 8, 1915, and made first vows two years later, on April 17, 1917.

---

[7] Gertrude Bodkin, RSCJ, born in Ireland in 1875, entered the Society at Roehampton, England, in 1894, a novice of Janet Erskine Stuart, RSCJ. She was finally professed at the then motherhouse in Paris in 1902 under Reverend Mother Mabel Digby. She came to New York in 1909 as mistress of novices and trained the next generation of RSCJ until 1931, when she became vicar of the New York Vicariate until 1953. She died October 18, 1966, a few hours before Louise Callan.

Formula of the Declaration to be signed by Postulants before their Clothing

I, the undersigned, Louise Callan ....having fully examined the Rules of the Congregation of the Religious of the Sacred Heart of Jesus, do hereby declare that I give them my entire adhesion.

Consequently, I ask to be admitted into the said Congregation, with the determination to consecrate myself therein to the service of God.

I bring to the Congregation nothing but the promise of my good will, and, I declare, that if for any cause whatsoever (whether through ill health or otherwise), I, leave of my own free will, or am forced to leave the said Congregation, will never claim any compensation for my services which call for no recompense.

In Witness Whereof, I have hereunto set my hand this ...13...day of

....April....19 15

IN PRESENCE OF

Louise Callan

Bodkin R.S.C.J.
a. E. Howe
r.s.c.j.

Document of renunciation signed as a postulant is clothed with the habit

6

Louise's first assignment was to Maryville Academy, on its old campus in South Saint Louis, where according to the community register, she arrived in August, 1917. Maryville was not to become a college until 1920, so the classes were at elementary and secondary level. In line with the kind of flexibility expected of young religious, she did different things each of her first four years. In her first year, 1917-1918, her musical talent was called on: she gave music lessons in piano and guitar. The next year, 1918-1919, she taught seventh grade English, First Academic (freshman) Algebra, and Latin IV. The third year, 1919-1920, she taught four subjects to the First Academic, and a course in College Latin, Readings in Livy. That was the first year that Maryville was moving toward college level. Again, typical of the kind of flexibility expected, the next year she was in the parish school teaching the eighth grade.

In October, 1920 she moved to the City House,[8] also in Saint Louis in the Central West End at Maryland and Taylor Streets. There she taught for the first three weeks of the fall semester in the Cathedral School, the parish elementary school of Saint Louis Cathedral Parish across Maryland Avenue, which RSCJ staffed briefly for five years, from 1916 to 1921. By November, however, she was assigned to the eighth grade at Barat Hall, the boys' school of the City House. It may have been a question of an urgent need to replace someone for the first weeks, or perhaps for the whole year, since her stay there lasted only one academic year. At the end of the school year 1920-1921, she was back at Maryville, August, 1921, teaching Latin classes in summer school, and during the school year Physics, Latin I and II, and other classes with Second and Fourth Academic. This continued for two years.

During this time, she earned a Bachelor of Arts degree from Saint Louis University, awarded in 1921. When she enrolled at the university, she received advanced standing for sixty-five college credits from the College of the Sacred Heart, Clifton, Cincinnati, and thirty-five from

---

[8] The "City House" (as opposed to the original foundations in Saint Charles and rural Florissant) was founded by Saint Philippine Duchesne in 1827 in South Saint Louis as academy, day school, and orphanage. It moved to the Central West End location in 1893, where it added Barat Hall School for boys, and closed in 1968.

Kenwood Normal Training School, Albany, New York. These latter were courses done during the "white juniorate," the second year of novitiate. The rest of the courses would have been taken during the summers, including six further credits from summer school 1912 at the University of Tennessee, before she entered, and two in the Ward Method of teaching music from Maryville in 1919. After forty further credits at Saint Louis University, she was awarded the degree in August, 1921. Her prowess in Latin had begun at Clifton with courses in Cicero and Virgil, and continued at Saint Louis University with Livy and Latin Composition. No major is given on her college transcript, but the greatest number of courses was taken in English, Latin, and Philosophy.

Passport photo and description on the way to Probation, 1922

By this time she was ready for "probation," the time of extended retreat in preparation for final profession. For this, she traveled to Rome with visas in her passport for Gibraltar and France, so they must also have stopped there. Her passport, including her signature on it, gives her name as Anna Louise; she is elsewhere Anne Louise, or later, just Louise. In Rome she began the program on September 12, 1922, at the motherhouse on Via Nomentana in the northeast corner of Rome. The director of the probation was Reverend Mother Vicente, assistant general during the term of Very Reverend Mother de Loë as superior general. Louise was organist. She hated pieces with seven flats. Once while she was struggling with one of them, a breeze came in the window and blew the music over the balcony onto the head of Reverend Mother Vicente. It was, however, typical of the strange situations in which Louise often found herself all her life. One day she was walking on the roof of the motherhouse building, where the nuns often walked, and saw a large number of troops marching down the street outside, the Via Nomentana. She called all the Americans there with her to come and look. Nothing was ever said about it. Later, she learned that it was Mussolini taking control of Rome! Nevertheless, she got through the probation program, which ended with final profession on February 10, 1923.

By the next month, she was back at Clifton, where she had been a student. Here she remained until September, 1926. During the first months that concluded the academic year, she filled in what was needed, principally as portress, the religious responsible for receiving visitors and keeping a record of comings and goings. She also taught Latin in the college. For the next academic year, 1923-1924, she taught Third Academic (high school junior) classes and Geometry (which no transcript indicates that she had every studied!), and the next two years, 1924-1926, Second Academic (sophomores) and Algebra. Then for the next two years, 1926-1928, it was back to Maryville in Saint Louis, where she was again to be found in the Third Academic classroom, and as organist and director of chapel singing. Meanwhile during the summers she was working on her Master of Arts at Saint Louis University, which she received in June, 1928. This time her major was History, with minors in Education and Latin. Her Master's thesis would prepare her for the work ahead: "The Political Regime of the French in the Mississippi Valley (1673-1763)."

The autumn of that year found her at Saint Charles, where she continued secondary school teaching and music: Fourth Academic (seniors) 1928-1932, organist and director of music. During the last two years, she was also mistress of studies, the equivalent of principal. In the listing of her ministries later compiled by her, she gives this title in French: *chargée des études*. That year she also taught Chemistry; this entry in her ministry record is followed by "!!!!!" – an apparent indication of what she thought of the idea. Besides this, she was studying German, undoubtedly to meet a language requirement for the doctorate in History, on which she was now working.

She did not remain at Saint Charles, but in 1932 she moved to Villa Duchesne in Saint Louis County for only one year. Here she taught

Third Academic (junior) Latin II, and Third Preparatory (seventh grade) Arithmetic. Her gifts in language, music, and mathematics seem to have been recognized during these years, and she was once more *chargée des études*, this time not only for the local school but for the Vicariate, which included six schools in Missouri, Ohio, and Louisiana. Meanwhile, when she had nothing else to do, she was taking doctoral classes at Saint Louis University. The next year, she was allowed to spend the majority of her time in studies, living at the City House, the community closest to Saint Louis University, for only one year, though: 1934-1936 found her back at Maryville, which had begun college courses in 1920. Louise now taught at the college level, and in the first year she continued to be in charge of studies for the schools of the Vicariate.

She had been admitted to doctoral candidacy in 1926 while still taking courses for the Masters, so it is difficult to sort out on her transcripts which courses were master's level and which doctoral. For the doctoral degree, her major was Modern European History, with minors in American History and Education. Over the entire program, of thirty-one courses taken in History, eleven were in North American History, the rest in European History and several Methods courses. Her doctoral dissertation was to become her first book: "History of the Society of the Sacred Heart in North America." Because of cloister, she was not allowed to travel for research unless she happened to be somewhere for other reasons, e.g., a history conference, so she wrote to every house of the Society for information. She received the Ph.D. in May, 1935. In the dissertation, she thanks Msgr. George P. Donnelly, chancellor of the archdiocese of Saint Louis for facilitating research in the archdiocesan archives, so she was permitted to go there for research in spite of cloister. The dissertation committee is not clearly given, but she thanks Rev. William J. McGucken, S.J., "for inspiration and aid," and Rev. Raymond Corrigan, S.J., "whose scholarly direction and patient encouragement made possible the completion of the work."[9]

---

[9] The dissertation is accessible on microfilm (T-433) in the Saint Louis University library and in paper in the University archives. Thanks to Juliet Mousseau, RSCJ, for this research.

MOTHER CALLAN, AUTHOR AND COLLEGE PROFESSOR

After Louise had completed the dissertation, Fathers Corrigan and Garraghan went to see Reverend Mother Mary Reid, superior vicar in Saint Louis, to tell her that she must allow Louise to make this into a book that would be published. Reverend Mother Reid agreed—she would have been hard put to resist two prominent Jesuit historians. The book was published in 1937 by Longmans, Green and Company of London/New York/Toronto under the title *The Society of the Sacred Heart in North America*. In the acknowledgements, Louise thanks three Jesuits. The first is Rev. Gilbert J. Garraghan, S.J., soon after to be author of a major publication, *The Jesuits of the Middle United States*,[10] "at whose suggestion the work was first undertaken and through whose courtesy it is being introduced to the reading public." His learned introduction to Louise's book, written from New York, reveals his close knowledge of its contents, but his actual relationship to its writing is not clear. The second is Father McGucken of Saint Louis University, who is thanked for "stimulating inspiration and valuable aid" with helpful "comments and criticism, as the writing progressed." The third is Father Corrigan "of the same institution." To him, "more than to anyone else, I make grateful acknowledgement for the wise counsel, scholarly direction and unflagging interest with which he followed the rough drafting and preparation of each chapter, and for the patient encouragement which sustained the effort required for the completion of the work." Readers and thesis director are not stated either in the book or university records, but it does sound as if Father Corrigan was the director and Father McGucken a reader. Father Garraghan was at the time socius

---

[10] 3 vols.; New York: J.J. Little and Ives, 1938; reprint Chicago: Loyola University Press, 1983.

(executive assistant) to the provincial superior of the Jesuit Missouri Province, and was teaching and chairing the Department of History at Saint Louis University, and he may well have been the second reader of the dissertation, though he is not acknowledged in it.[11] Father Corrigan, more than anyone else, provided support and encouragement to Louise through the long haul of dissertation writing and preparation of the manuscript for publication.

The book was received with widespread acclaim. The *Historical Bulletin*, Saint Louis, of March 1938 hailed it as "an exhaustive treatment, well documented, and at the same time presented in a very agreeable and fascinating way….Its pages teem with vivid detail, interesting to the lay reader scarcely less than to the religious." The *Pulpit Digest* of the same month called it "a notable success…which will undoubtedly become the standard work on the subject….indispensable to anyone interested in religious and educational progress in our country. The scholarship in research, clarity in presentation and brilliant treatment make this history eminently readable." Similarly, Jerome T. Boyle, S.J., in the *Denver Register* of 3.10.1938 claimed: "Here the scholar will find the most exacting standards of research, accurate documentation…while the general reader will delight in the imaginative and lively presentation of an unknown but significant phase of American history." The *Catholic Educational Review* (vol. 36 [3.19.1938] 187-88) called it "a scholarly, invaluable contribution," while R. Corrigan (presumably the Jesuit at Saint Louis University involved with the writing of the dissertation) suggested in *Mid-America* (vol. 9 [4.1938]143-44) that "it may serve as a model and inspiration to others."

The Society of the Sacred Heart in North America did indeed become a standard reference work, beginning with a brief introduction to the European background and the early life of Philippine Duchesne before her journey with four companions to the New World in 1818. Subsequent chapters trace the development of the Society's houses from Saint Louis to Louisiana to Sugar Creek, Kansas, New York, Pennsylvania, Canada and the northern and western United States, and

---

[11] Thanks to Juliet Mousseau, RSCJ, and David Miros of the Midwest Jesuit Archives for this research.

Mexico and the Caribbean. Each piece of the history is traced separately for the nineteenth century. The concluding chapters summarize events of the twentieth century as far as 1937, and the educational system of Sacred Heart schools as it was carried out in the early twentieth century. With the publication of the book, Louise's academic reputation as a historian was established.

Yet she was to spend three more years, 1937-1940, teaching English, History, Religion, Latin, and Chemistry at the Academy of the Sacred Heart in New Orleans, while also being organist and choir director. She arrived in New Orleans in August, 1937, just after her book had appeared. The students were very impressed that they had a Ph.D. and an author for teacher. She had the Fourth Academic (senior) class each year for their major subjects, and she was soon very popular with students and parents alike. In the summer of 1939, she taught three History courses at San Francisco College for Women, and by fall, 1940, she was at Maryville College in Saint Louis teaching History, Education, and Religion as well as responsible for organ and choir. She had no formal training in theology or Scripture, yet throughout her years at Maryville she taught in these areas, though she never felt completely confident.

By 1945, she had begun to think about a biography of Philippine Duchesne. With her beatification in 1940, more attention was being paid to the pioneer saint and a shrine in Saint Charles was being planned and built. There was not yet a complete in-depth biography.[12] It was a slow and laborious task. Louise had not been asked to do it but conceived of it on her own initiative. She had to fit in the research while she was carrying on the rest of her full-time work. She was not allowed to go to Rome to examine the originals of Philippine's letters. By this time, most of them had been transcribed by probanists, and typed copies were sent to her of the letters that she requested, so she

---

12 Abbé Baunard, author of the first published biography of Saint Madeleine Sophie, had also written a shorter but full biography of Philippine Duchesne (*Histoire de Mme. Duchesne*, Paris, 1878), translated into English by Lady Georgiana Fullerton in 1879 and re-issued in French paperback in 1940 as the "beatification edition." The only other extended biography yet published was that of Marjory Erskine, RSCJ, *Mother Philippine Duchesne* (New York: Longmans, Green, and Co., 1926).

was completely reliant on the accuracy of the transcribers, who were by no means professional, and moreover, she had to know about the existence of a letter in order to request the transcription. It has also since become evident that what she was given was censored.[13] Anything in the correspondence that may have reflected badly on another RSCJ, for example, Eugénie Audé[14] or Elisabeth Galitzine,[15] was not sent. In later

[13] A letter of Louise Vétillart, RSCJ, then an assistant in the general secretariat, to Superior General Reverend Mother Thérèse de Lescure, dated June 6, 1953, reports that Louise had already received from the general archives copies of all the letters that had been transcribed by probanists, and that she was now asking for others that were extant in manuscript only and because of their sensitivity, could not be given to probanists to transcribe. In the opinion of the author of the letter, they would not be directly relevant to the biography. After discussion with Reverend Mother de Lescure, she added a note to the letter to the effect that Mother Callan would be told that everything that could be sent to her already was sent, and that anything that remained belonged to the "secret archive" reserved to the superior general. (Society of the Sacred Heart General Archives, Rome)

[14] Eugénie Audé was born in Moutiers, France in 1791. She entered the Society in Grenoble in 1815 and made first vows in 1817. She was chosen as one of the four companions of Philippine to America, and made her final profession on February 8, 1818—the morning of their departure from Paris. With American novice Mary Layton she was founder at Grand Coteau in 1821 and at Saint Michaels in 1825. Supposedly subject to Philippine as superior, she instead acted very independently of Philippine's authority. In 1833 she was named assistant general for America. She visited all the American houses, then went to France, from which she never returned. She was later superior at the Trinità dei Monti in Rome, where she died in 1842. She is buried under the high altar of the church.

[15] Elizabeth Galitzine (or Galitzin) was born in 1795 into a family of the Russian nobility and Russian Orthodox faith, converted to Roman Catholicism by Jesuits in Saint Petersburg. She entered the Society in 1828 in Rome and was professed in 1832. She was secretary general at the General Council in 1839, there named provincial for America. She visited all the American houses in 1840, relieved Mother Duchesne of her position as superior (which she had long sought), and made many changes, some of which were later regretted. Realizing her role in the Society's crisis of 1839, she returned to America in 1843 to revisit the places where she had disseminated the changes mandated there. She died of yellow fever at Saint Michaels during that journey.

years, it was hard on her to know that others were allowed to access the original materials in Rome and thus had information that she did not have. Her correspondence with the motherhouse during these years includes pages of lists of dates and recipients of the letters she asked for. What she accomplished within these limits was remarkable. She *was* allowed to go with two college students as "chaperones" to the old Saint Ferdinand convent in Florissant, where Philippine and companions had moved their whole *ménage* from Saint Charles in 1819. One later recalled that as they walked across the field, Louise said: "This must be the place where the cow wouldn't move."

On her summary of activities, she notes for 1945-1951, "trying to write." From January to July, 1952, she was given relief from teaching and moved to the City House in the Central West End of Saint Louis where she could devote herself to writing with no teaching "except substituting." Her location at the City House gave her freedom from the fast pace of college life and must have allowed her easier access to the Saint Louis University libraries. By autumn of 1952, she was back at the college with teaching, writing, and as organist.

Quite surprising to her, Louise found so much material to incorporate in this first historical biography of Mother Duchesne that the manuscript grew larger than any publisher was willing to accept. One of the Maryville students at the time, Marge Seitz, later RSCJ, remembers helping her cut the manuscript. Still, the final product came to over eight hundred pages. An *Imprimatur* was granted for the book in 1954, but it did not appear until 1957: *Philippine Duchesne: Frontier Missionary of the Sacred Heart 1769-1852.* Westminster, Maryland: The Newman Press.

MEMORIES OF STUDENTS
AND COMMUNITY

Louise was so musically gifted that she could play anything on piano, organ, or guitar. Once when in charge of a high school recreation, she came with a guitar to play and sing. A student who was there said that it gave her an entirely different view of the Society. At the old Maryville, Louise's classroom was on the second floor just to the side of the chapel, and her little office off the classroom had a window that opened onto the chapel. It was also near the organ loft, and she was organist and choir director. She composed her own choir hymnal for use of the choir. She was very much updated on the burgeoning liturgical movement and was ready to adjust to the new ways of liturgical practice that were coming in in the 1950s. All the leaders in the student body were in the choir, so it was a powerful group and the place where you found out what was happening among the students. Often before Sunday afternoon Benediction, students in the choir would arrive early and find her in prayer on the prie-dieu near the organ. On the day of a birthday of one of the choir members, Louise would improvise "Happy Birthday" on the organ at Communion, so subtly that others not in the choir did not catch on. During the student retreat, she would insist on one and one-half hours of choir practice daily. The first fifteen minutes would be choir practice, and the rest was sing-along, to let off steam. One year the retreat was particularly dreadful and the students were angry. Louise said nothing, but that year added dancing as well as singing during choir practice. One of her choir remembered:

I can never think of Mother Callan in any more vivid way than that posture of intensity that she assumed whenever she was setting our worship to music. She seemed transported by the very effort of producing a sound that was uplifting and appropriate to the occasion. Then, at other times, she would

16

comply with the requests of the girls whose high school days in Sacred Heart schools had exposed them to the cherished strains of "Cœur de Jésus" or "When the Battle Rages Fiercest." And, with that characteristic twinkle in her eye, she would give them what they begged for. We were of one accord as we sang "Qui Donc Es-Tu?" on December 8, "Beau Ciel" on Ascension Thursday, or "O Beata" on November 17.[16]

Louise was a great teacher who inspired her students to work prodigiously. "Love, enthusiasm, and academic perfectionism joined forces with a keen sense of humor." One remembered that her American History class "was like being there." She was an incredible story teller, and vivacious, all over the room as she talked. When she called the roll of a class, each name was pronounced carefully and reverently. Already in the 1950s she was teaching development of doctrine in her theology classes. Only later did some of those students realize how important this was and what a foundation it gave them for what was to come.

Every year for the feast of Philippine, Louise put up signs to collect money from the students for "candy for the Potawatomi" and sent it off somewhere, they never knew where. Nearly everyone who ever lived with her in community remembers the "arabesque." One of her employments was as chaperone for the students who were taking dance class. She could mimic the arabesque movement perfectly, which she frequently did at community recreation and whenever called upon to do it.

---

[16] Remembrance of Jane Cannon. The songs referenced here are all traditional Society hymns with the exception of "O Beata," composed by Academy of the Sacred Heart, Saint Charles, music teacher Kasper Theissen on the occasion of Philippine's beatification in 1940.

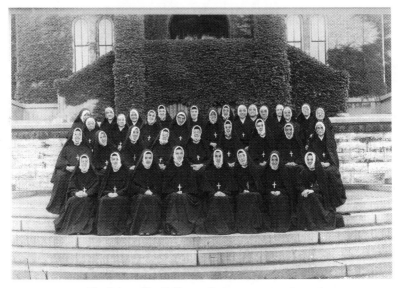

The Maryville College religious community at
the old Maryville College circa 1948
Louise is in first row, third from right.
Photo by Marie Kernaghan, RSCJ

Sometimes trusted college students were asked to go along on car trips as she visited Saint Charles, Florissant, etc. for historical research. Added to the usual prayers for a safe journey was a prayer to Saint Patrick for green lights. One pair of such students found themselves for a few moments alone with the other accompanying person, a lay history teacher, who told them that Louise was esteemed as one of the finest historians. They already thought she walked on water, but now they had more to admire in her.

The students totally loved her and innocently did not hesitate to demonstrate their affection, of a kind not shown to their other teachers, nearly all of whom were religious. In the atmosphere of religious life in the 1950s and early 1960s, such "singularity" sometimes attracted disapproval from authority, though her peers and those who lived with her in community were seldom resentful. Louise was known for her deep compassion and total generosity, without calculation. Yet she was sometimes mistrusted by authority and even publicly humiliated. Once when she offered a comment at community recreation, she was told by a superior in front of the whole community that one of her ideas was too grand, "as they always are." When she used expressions like "heart-sorrow" or "heart-loneliness" to describe Philippine, some thought it was as if she was talking about herself. She was not a conformist, but was perceived by some as something of a maverick; she always had her own way of doing things. "I don't run with the pack, dear," she was known to say.

She had a great deal of nervous energy, and even when exhausted and in pain, she could keep working for long hours. One community member remembers her as one of the most gifted and one of the most difficult in community life. She had a quick temper that would sometimes explode unexpectedly, but she would always apologize later. In her last years, when she was suffering a great deal, she sometimes responded to the question, how are you, with "I'm fine for someone with five mortal illnesses!"

In the mid-1960s, a large group of young religious was in the community at Maryville in the new program of "Doctrinal Formation," legislated by the General Chapter of 1964. They were to spend up to three years after first vows in theological study before being sent to teach. The program lasted only a few years before falling by the wayside, but the group who were making first vows then participated in it—to the envy of those who had made vows only a year or two earlier and were laboring in the classrooms of other schools. Those in Doctrinal Formation from the Chicago and Saint Louis Vicariates who did not have a college degree or lacked adequate undergraduate theology courses were at Maryville.

It was customary to have a book read during the noon meal, and the reader was usually one of the young religious. Louise had charge of preparing the readers for their work. When a word was mispronounced, Louise would gasp audibly. There was one memorable incident of those years, about 1965, remembered by everyone who was present. Some think the very book being read may have been Louise's biography of Philippine, but that is unlikely as it would already have been published for a number of years. In any event, there were a number of references to "quais," correctly pronounced like "kays." The reader pronounced the word "kways." When Louise was displeased, it was evident not only from the gasp, but also in her body language and the increasing redness of her face. The reader could tell that Louise was unhappy, but she did not know why. All of a sudden, Louise half rose from her seat and blurted out: "Sister! It's 'kays'!" Everyone in the refectory was somewhat taken aback, so Reverend Mother Mulqueen[17] ended the reading for the day. The next day, the same reader was back reading the continuation of the same passage. When she came upon the word, she said "kays—which yesterday were kways." This time, the whole room burst out laughing, and Louise joined in the laughter.

Some of the senior community members who were college professors and very busy had the habit of coming to the late afternoon community recreation only for a few minutes, standing in the back of the room while the rest of the community were seated in a semicircle. They would wait to see if there was any news they needed to know, and then leave quietly. It was customary at community recreation to pass a box of candy around so that each person present could take a piece. Louise was known to wait not only for news, but also for the candy to come around to her. The young sister whose room was directly across from hers often found it on her bed.

A young religious who lived at the old Maryville with Louise was a terrible speller, and everyone knew it. Once at recreation, the superior announced that Mother O'Byrne from Manhattanville was coming to visit, with Mother McDonnell. There was question of which one, as there were two of that name in the New York Vicariate and two in the Washington Vicariate, but with different spellings. The young religious asked if it had one 'n' or two. "What difference does that make," someone queried? The young nun replied: "You spell Alice with one 'n'" – meaning that Alice McDonell's *last* name was spelled with one

---

[17] Eleanor Mulqueen, born in New York City in 1897, entered the Society in 1917 and was professed in 1925. From 1940-1964, she was superior at Elmhurst, 91st St., Manhattanville, and Kenwood. In 1963 she was superior at Maryville, and from 1964-1969, vicar of the Saint Louis Vicariate. She was also local superior at Maryville at the time of Louise's death. She died at Kenwood in 1992.

'n,' McDonell. There was dead silence in the room until finally Louise said: "Honey, even you can't spell Alice with one 'n'!"

Sr. Marie Kernaghan[18] was a notable person in the Maryville community, Professor of Science, first woman to get a Ph.D. at Saint Louis University, and a member of the Catholic Commission for Cultural and Intellectual Affairs (CCICA). Mother Kernaghan could wax eloquent about her activities, and once in awhile, Louise would come out with "Now, Mother..." to bring her down if she started flying too high. Behind the scenes, Louise was also heard to sing "Oh say can you CCICA"!

---

[18] Marie Kernaghan, RSCJ, was born in New Orleans in 1889. She entered the Society at Kenwood in 1908 and made final profession in 1916. She taught for 61 years at Maryville (1915-1976), first in the Academy, then at the college level from 1919. Saint Louis University did not accept women students until 1926, so by special arrangement with the Jesuits, she earned the B.A. in 1921 and M.A. in 1925 in Physics and Math, receiving her diploma by mail. She earned the Ph.D. in Physics in 1929. She died in Saint Charles in 1985.

THE LECTURES ON
MOTHER DUCHESNE

By the 1950s Louise had hit her stride as a teacher and writer, though she did not have time to write much beyond the massive biography on which she was working. She was well known by this time as a competent historian, a member of the American Historical Association, the American Catholic Historical Association, the Mississippi Valley Historical Society, and the Missouri Historical Society.

During these years when Louise was working on the Duchesne biography, word got out about her project, and she was often asked to give lectures on "Blessed Philippine" in Sacred Heart communities, schools, and for alumnae and friends. Between 1951 and 1957, she gave such lectures in Chicago, Detroit, Cincinnati, New Orleans; in Greenwich and Noroton, Connecticut; in Albany, Rochester, and New York City, New York, and many in the Saint Louis area, including to the Saint Charles County Historical Society in October, 1957. Many of these presentations have been preserved, mostly without date or place. They are her own typed texts, often with corrections or annotations written in. The lectures gave Louise the chance to develop aspects of Philippine Duchesne that she could only hint at in a historical biography. She portrays Philippine as a lively child directing the play of her younger siblings and cousins, enjoying being a teenager with her cousin Josephine, as a special friend of younger children at Sainte Marie,[19] a community member upon whom others could always rely, and "a free-lance social worker" during the middle years in Grenoble before 1804. Philippine is called "a soul of unlimited desires."

---

[19] The Visitation Monastery of Sainte Marie-d'en-Haut in Grenoble, France, was the place where Saint Philippine Duchesne attended boarding school, entered the Visitation order as a novice, acquired after the French Revolution, turned over to Saint Madeleine Sophie in 1804, and spent the next eleven years of her life.

One of these presentations that does carry a date was to the A.A.S.H. (Associated Alumnae/Alumni of the Sacred Heart) National Conference at her old school, Convent of the Sacred Heart, Clifton, Cincinnati, on May 25, 1951. She begins with the quip: "It is a rather amazing experience for me to be invited to speak in the very room in which, long ago, I was so frequently requested to stop talking." The theme of her presentation follows upon Father Gavan-Duffy's frequently noted question in his little booklet *Heart of Oak,* "What have we learned from her?" In response, Louise asks the question, "What have we failed to realize about Philippine Duchesne?" She notes that we have associated her with

> strength, endurance, austerity; with burning zeal for souls, and patience under trial and failure; with a certain severity of manner and outlook, and complete detachment from the earthly things we cling to so tenaciously. All this is great and noble, fine and true, as far as it goes, but it is a very one-sided view of the Society's great frontier heroine.

The rest of the lecture highlights Philippine's warm, loving, and enduring relationships with her family, her experiences growing up in the large extended family of the Periers and the Duchesnes, and especially with her brother Hippolyte and her beloved cousin, Josephine Perier de Savoye-Rollin.

Someone who was a young religious in the Clifton community at the time remembered that Louise thought the community needed cheering up, so she asked if community recreation one evening of her visit could be in the parlor, where the piano was. She took to the piano and had the whole community singing along and laughing.

On December 29, 1952, Louise addressed the American Catholic Historical Association in Washington, DC, in the centenary year of Philippine's death. The paper charts the main events of her life. Toward the end, one glimpses the intimacy and a certain identification that Louise felt with Philippine by this time:

> In youth she had been fired as with wild desires, impetuous and at times imperious. In old age the calm of a distant

outlook towards the horizons of eternity had settled down upon her soul, but had not deadened the keen sensitiveness that caused her personal suffering all her life. She bore the burden and responsibility of the Society's first missionary venture for twenty-two years, and her position as Superior through that long period was one of her greatest trials. It seemed to give her claim in her own eyes to the hardest work, the worst accommodations, the poorest clothing, the most meager nourishment, and the longest hours of prayer – for under the pressure of work and pain, loneliness and failure, she turned always to converse with God. The night hours were her favorite time for prayer before the Blessed Sacrament, when she strengthened her spirit by deep draughts of the Divine. And we who reap the harvest she sowed know the tremendous power of her inspiration.

The talk concludes with reference to the newly built shrine in Saint Charles:

> Her spirit seems to dwell in the little convent at Saint Charles, Missouri, where she spent the last decade of her holy life in ever deepening seclusion. There a new memorial shrine is rising above her mortal remains, a symbol of the appreciation and veneration felt by the Church and the Society of the Sacred Heart, its alumnae and pupils and friends throughout the world, for Blessed Philippine Duchesne.

In an article for *Sponsa Regis* (30:8, April, 1959, pp. 193-202), Louise has room to speculate on what Philippine and her beloved cousin Josephine Perier were like as teenagers, a portrait of Philippine again unlike the usual one:

> Almost the same age, they grew up like twins, had the same governess, went to boarding school together, received First Communion and Confirmation together, planned their lives in confidence together, and the bond of their friendship lasted

until Josephine's death in 1850. As teen-agers they wore pretty clothes, silk stockings, fine gloves and shoes, big hats, graceful capes on the street, and shawls. They went to parties, concerts, dances, and there were interesting escorts. They took dancing lessons, music lessons, art.

Later as a nun at Sainte Marie, Philippine is portrayed as friend to small children:

> She was the special friend of the younger children, who used to get into trouble quite often. When they got in too deep, she took over until the storm subsided. She knew how to handle them and put them back on the path of good conduct, and they loved her with a kind of worship. She was very vivacious, full of initiative, gay and interesting with the children, a leader in their games and recreations. She always had things to talk to them about, and one thing most of all: foreign missions all over the world were her pet theme, her great ambition.

In an undated talk given in Saint Charles, Louise waxes eloquent about Philippine in America. One senses deep levels of identification with the rise and fall of hope in Louise's own life.

> She knew the mighty Mississippi and the turbulent Missouri, knew their fog and fever, their treacherous current and unpredictable course, their seasons of freeze and flood. She experienced the changing fortunes of pioneer life, now heart-warming, now heart-breaking, its time of soaring hope alternating with spells of drab depression, for which only heroic faith and love could muster grim determination to carry on.

Louise's well-balanced imagination was able to create images of Philippine that showed the many aspects of her personality, even as her descriptions subtly but surely incorporated the aspirations of Louise herself.

THE VIEW THROUGH
RELATIONSHIP

During these years a special relationship developed with Margaret Byrne, R.C., who saved many of Louise's letters from 1952 to 1966. She was not able to save all of them; earlier in her own formation program, she was under a rule to read personal letters and discard them. The letters that remain chronicle the events of Louise's life at this time. They also reveal her as a warm, affectionate, and sometimes irreverent commentator on life around her. They show her loves, her preoccupations, and increasingly as she aged and battled with cancer, her strong spirit and heroic endurance of chronic pain, even while she was admired by those who lived with her and benefited from her teaching.

Margaret, some years younger than Louise, was a student at the Rosary in New Orleans when Louise was teaching there 1937-1940. Later she spent three semesters as a college student at Maryville before entering the Religious of the Cenacle. The bond between the two of them was lifelong. The original idea when Margaret entered religious life was that they would write each First Friday, but this was not possible for Margaret during formation. The timing of the letters adjusted to what was possible. Later, when Margaret was superior in various locations, both had the freedom to write often. When Margaret as a young religious went to Rome for her tertianship before final profession, Louise reminisced about her own memories of Rome, as she wrote on September 22, 1952:

Dearest Meg,

I thought you were lost on the way home. So you went to Milwaukee as well as Chicago. Well, join the order and see the world! I was so glad to have your letter, even if you failed to give me the sailing date, pier, boat, line, etc. Very well, no flowers, fruit, or candy shall I send you! We had registration last week. 125 freshmen! More than 300 in the college! God is good—maybe we can pay our debts! The drain we had to put in was a terrific non-budgeted expense, you know. Classes began today. I have 3 American history courses, and one Religion section I did not expect—but even with 4 sections the classes are too large. I have 36! The choir promises well. We are offering education courses on Saturday mornings and expect many nuns as well as teachers.... Reverend M. McCabe[20] flew from Boston with Rev. M. Barry[21] last night. They are in Rome tonight, and you will be there soon, too. I am so happy for you. It is a very great grace, Meg. I can only pray that your tertianship may mean as much to you as mine meant to me, and that the long retreat may be as heavenly, not full of sweets one can taste but of strength one can lean on. I do so hope you go to visit Mater, and the Scala Sancta, and St. Praxedes where the pillar of the scourging is, and St. Cecilia's, and St. Agnes with its catacombs (out beyond our Maison Mère on Via Nomentana), and St. Paul's Outside the Walls, and the Lateran, besides the Vatican and St. Peter's. Take me along at every step and renew my spiritual youth. I am growing older than you realize. You are just the age I was when I went to probation 30 years ago [August, 1922-March, 1923] with profession in Feb. 1923....

The days of your visit were like a dream—but I know they were a reality—you can never know how deeply I appreciated the permission for you to stop a while with me, and the joy of seeing you so well, so happy, so mature, so womanly, so yourself with it all. Only the best religious training can give all that.

---

[20] Angela McCabe, RSCJ, was born in Saint Louis in 1888, entered the Society in 1916, and was professed in 1924. She was superior vicar of the Saint Louis Vicariate 1944-1963, and died at Saint Charles in 1982.

[21] Agnes Barry, RSCJ, was born in Rochester, New York, in 1893. She entered the Society in 1912 and was professed in 1920. She was superior vicar of the Washington Vicariate 1950-1966, and died at Kenwood in 1979.

There was so much left unsaid on both sides of the road![22] But we are closer than ever in the Heart of Christ. May He bless you and may Our Lady keep you safe forever. You know with what love I am

Your old mother in C.J.
Louise Callan r.s.c.j.

One year later, on September 5, 1953, another "across the road" visit took place, when Margaret, newly professed, was given responsibility in formation as director of postulants:

> Just to think of it! We had a second visit "across the road" sooner than I had dared hope for. It was a very great joy for me. God is so good to us, Meg....
>
> And in three weeks Our Very Reverend Mother [de Valon][23] will be at Maryville. She arrives Sept. 28 at 4 P.M. on our threshold! Can you hear me practicing the chorus of 300 voices for the reception in the gym? No tableaux or dialogue, just an address in French and some super-fine music! And just *one week* in which to practice the students one hour a day. Pray that all goes well. I shall write you all about it in Oct.

My class schedule is light, just 8 hrs. a week – so I *must* finish the book.... You realize that I shall try to help you with my best prayers. May Our Lady show you how to train true R.C.'s from the very day of their entrance. I beg you not to be tense, not to *notice* everything you see. Try to show them how to *relax fervently*! And how to find the answer to all their problems in love for the Sacred Heart, our all.

---

[22] The Cenacle Retreat House was located just across Spoede Road from Villa Duchesne, a Sacred Heart school in Saint Louis County. Louise sometimes got permission to go to Villa and Margaret would cross the road to visit.

[23] Sabine de Valon, RSCJ, was superior general 1958-1967. As president of the International Union of Superiors General, she was an auditor at the later sessions of Vatican II. It was during her generalate that many of the changes in religious life happened. She died in Lyon in 1990.

Margaret Byrne, RC, and Louise Callan, RSCJ,
at one of their meetings sometime in the 1950s
Photo in the Maryville *Alumnae News*, November, 1966

In 1953, an unexpected shadow had crossed Louise's path: cancer was discovered. If she already knew when writing this letter, she gives no sign. She had surgery in the summer of 1954, probably a mastectomy. The following year she remained at Maryville during recovery and retained organ and choir but taught no classes. The surgery permanently altered the freedom of arm movement; from then on, she held up one arm with the other when she wrote on the blackboard. By 1955 she had added three classes to her activities, and the next year, six courses. The cancer continued to follow her, though, for the rest of her life.

After praising a new vocation brochure written by Margaret, she makes a small allusion to her new disability on May 6, 1956:

Dearest Meg,

Have your ears been burning lately? Well, of course I'm no judge, I'm prejudiced in your favor, but Mother Bascom is objective and good at criticism, and I can not get my precious copy of your beautiful booklet back from her....I read the first section to Mother Shaw (she's nearly blind now)[24] and she kept on saying "How beautiful!" "Read that again"....Mother Bascom is hard to please and, Meg o'my heart, *her is pleased.* Of course I'm swollen with pride and thrilled with joy....

I just scribble with this new kind of pen, but I can write pretty well on the blackboard now. The nerve contractions will never relax, they say, so I have my hair shirt for life—but I also know I have His love.

Two weeks later, on May 20, she has a few critiques of Margaret's booklet to raise, the result of its being read in the refectory to the college RSCJ community, then she says:

> Yesterday I went to the Alumnae meeting at St. Charles with Mother Happy.[25] She was in the academy there before coming to Maryville for college. I spoke on Bl. Philippine after the luncheon. It was a very good meeting – almost double the number in former years – and they are all so interested in the A.A.S.H. meeting in St. Louis and St. Charles in 1957, May 1-4. We hope to get the book out for that. Mr. McHale of Newman Press let me down in the matter of publication for Christmas 1956, as he had suggested at first. Well, there is no use worrying about it....God has some meaning for me in all this delay and handicap and crippled arm and the rest. I try to rest in His Will – it is the only place to rest. Sometimes I think quite piously about it all – imagine me being

---

[24] This was Mother Cora Shaw, the mistress general in Cincinnati who had been so influential in Louise's childhood. She was infirm at this time and died at Maryville two years later, on January 1, 1958.

[25] Corinne Bertha Happy, RSCJ, was born in Saint Charles, Missouri in 1901. She attended the Academy of the Sacred Heart there, then two years at Maryville. After two more years of working, she entered the Society at Kenwood in 1922, making first vows in 1925. She was finally professed there in 1931. She served in every house of the then Saint Louis Vicariate/ Province in many forms of service, notably infirmarian and treasurer. She was known for her selfless service to all. It was said of her after her death that "she literally wore herself out in the Lord's service." She died in Saint Charles in 1983.

pious! *Laeva eius sub capite meo et dextera illius amplexabitur me.*[26] That right hand of His reached right around me in an embrace of love and left the pain to remind me of that love. But I am still very cowardly about it – I should so love to wake up and find I could move without the pain – but I have it on very good authority and not on any conclusion of my own: the pain is here to stay – and you'd never suspect it if you saw me. I look "like a million dollars" – or whatever that means….and I am very well.

A few weeks later, on June 15, the chronic pain is still something that she struggles to brush off:

Well, we all have to get old. I am all right – no need to worry – just pray that I make use of the thing – I really do not appreciate it as I should. I know it is "a gift of God" but I am always hoping it will let up. At present they are trying electric nerve-and-muscle stimulator shock treatment on it at St. Anthony's Hospital twice a week. Waste of time and money – no sign of relief. I could take a kind of pain-killer like heroin compound – but not if I can help it – I might "get the habit" – then what? Codeine compounds are of no use – no more than starch! Why worry? I am well enough.

The hoped for appearance of the biography for May did not materialize. A year later, on June 16, 1957, she is increasingly being called on for her expertise about Blessed Philippine, but is still awaiting the appearance of the biography:

I was ending the fourth week of my so-beautiful and so-helpful and so-prayerful retreat… (and I had got that far this afternoon when the executone called me "Mother Curran[27] on

---

[26] His left hand is under my head and his right hand will embrace me. *Song of Songs* 2:6; 8:3.

[27] Matilde Neil Curran, RSCJ, born in Sedalia, Missouri in 1891, professed in 1927, was vicariate secretary, so this message came from the superior vicar, Reverend Mother Angela McCabe. Mother Curran died at Saint Charles in 1983.

the phone" – so off I went two hours ago to learn that I may accept an invitation to give three talks on Blessed Ph.D. in Chicago come September 27-31 – alumnae and student groups at the two convents there. Last week I got an order for a copy of the new book for the Cenacle in Milwaukee…I wish I had a copy of that book. Not a sign of a page to proof-read YET – and the book is advertised now to appear in September. I am disillusioned about these excellent, high-standard Catholic publishers – who give no contract, break their word, only hold you to pay the bill….Enough!

....Mother Bush[28] is here teaching in the Summer School, a course on Methods of Teaching English in High School. She uses me at times to try out her ideas on. The other day she asked me if I use the Unit Method. Of course I acted dumber than usual and asked what a unit was – she said, "Why, a WHOLE, of course" – So I smiled brightly and said, "O yes, indeed; I teach many a H-O-L-E – what did she do? She used that to introduce her class next day. So one of the young nuns told me – and Mother Bush added, by way of precaution to her Juniors: "O course, if Mother Callan does not use the unit method it is because she just teaches, and she has been at it long enough to use her own methods." Antique….

Teaching in the Summer School, even just a small class of young nuns, takes so much time – and I flatten out on the bed so often to get the old nerves to relax. I am ashamed of my cowardice about the pain – it does not get better but it is His Gift and His Will and He should get something out of it.

Later in the summer, August 28, she was still awaiting page proofs on the book, but going as a traveling companion to a professional political science meeting in New York, where she would be nearer to Margaret:

---

[28] Marie Adele Bush, RSCJ, was born in New Orleans in 1906 and professed in 1934. At this time she was mistress of studies in New Orleans. She died in Saint Charles in 1990.

What news of the book? I await the page proofs....

And by the way, could you drop me a postal to Convent of the Sacred Heart, #1 East 91st Street, N.Y. City, and tell me the best time to call you on Sunday morning, Sept. 8 – or after 6 P.M. on Sept. 4,5,6,7 – which is next week? I am going to N.Y. with Mother Barrett[29] for the meeting of the American Political Science Association, Sept. 5,6,7 – so we fly TWA on the 4th, and home on the afternoon of the 8th. It will be good to hear your dear voice for at least a few minutes. I shall be going to Chicago at the end of September for an alumnae meeting, to speak on Blessed Philippine. Very nice side line!

---

[29] Patricia Barrett, RSCJ, was born in Gary, Indiana in 1914, entered the Society in 1935, was professed at Kenwood in 1945, and was for many years Professor of Political Science at Maryville. She died at Oakwood, Atherton, California in 1987.

THE BIOGRAHY APPEARS AND SETS A FUTURE COURSE

The biography did finally appear, and praise for this exhaustive work was swift. The *Ligourian* of May, 1958 called it "an excellent historical and biographical work." Charles Van Ravenswaay in the *Saint Louis Post-Dispatch* of February 9, 1958, wrote: "The quietness and understatement of this volume will confuse many readers familiar with the usual historical biography." Henry Willmering, S.J., in *The Critic* said of the author that "in this biography Mother Callan is content to be an accompanist, who puts forth the value of the artist." John Francis Bannon in *America* for April 12, 1958, spoke of her "deep understanding and scholarship…" "a work worthy of the historian and one which the hagiographer should hail as a contribution to his library." Wm. T. Longust in *The Josephinum Review* of April 9, 1958, praised the book as being "of epic proportions," "a monumental work of impressive scholarship, a significant contribution to the history of the Church of the Midwest, and, above all, a work worthy of its subject." E. R. Vollmar, S.J., wrote in the *Saint Louis Review* that "this work is *the* biography. Publishers are given to exaggeration but this is one time when a reviewer can give full credit to the claim '…now that Mother Callan has written Philippine Duchesne there is nothing left to be done.' " Ralph F. Bayard in the *Catholic Historical Review* (vol. 44: 227-228. July, 1958) concurred: "She reveals, as no previous writer has done, the real Philippine Duchesne…she furnishes students of American church history with the open sesame to a treasure house of source material hitherto sealed in Roman archives….The use Mother Callan has made of her sources compels unstinted praise….Filial pruning and unobjective puffing have alike been scorned….The upshot of such expert handling is that Mother Duchesne emerges with satisfying completeness and consistent vividness through her journals and letters….(the book) appears to warrant the accolade 'definitive.'"

The relief of having the book out and the appreciative comments that were beginning to flow in were overshadowed by the pain of losing her childhood guide and now longtime friend and companion in community, Mother Cora Shaw, who died on January 1, 1958, at Maryville. The superior general of the Society, Marie-Thérèse de Lescure,[30] had died the previous day, December 31, 1957. Louise wrote on New Year's Day to Margaret Byrne:

> Our Mother General died last night and Mother Shaw died this morning as I knelt by her bed just after Communion. I am strangely numb – and have had such a hard week since Christmas day, when Mother Shaw had another stroke. She had a long hard week of dying – such a mystery. The funeral will be on the First Friday – I miss her dreadfully after being with her so much these past five years. But I am not sad – it is glorious to think of what she now possesses.
>
> I am very dull this afternoon – I can not find what I meant to write or send you. Never mind. So many people have said nice things about the book. God is so good. A last proof of His care is this: He allowed me to overlook mentioning the name of the young nun who designed the jacket for the book, and she has just left the Society – from third probation – at Kenwood – for reasons of health.

Between grieving the loss of Mother Shaw and coping with book reviews, she wrote on February 12, 1958, now with uncertainty about the future of Maryville:

> Dearest Meg,
>
> You cannot realize how much I appreciated that phone call. I just think you all are wonderful to me. I am not getting caught up with my mail at all – there was such a lot of extra

---

[30] Reverend Mother de Lescure had been superior general since 1946 and had visited the United States in 1953.

because of Mother Shaw – she had such a lot of friends who had to be informed and then thanked. Then I had to do an article for The Magazine on her and meet a deadline. Then there have been SO MANY kind people I had to thank – people I never heard from (or of) before, but who wrote nice things about the book. So forgive me for being so slow about writing. Here are a few reviews and letters. Send them back some day – no hurry. I lost the one out of the *Times Picayune* for January 26. Sorry! It was nice enough until the end – then came the blow, to the effect that the Indians summed up Mother Duchesne in four words, "Woman who prays always" – but it took the author 745 pages to do so! It is fun reading what they have to say....
Pray for me during Lent very specially – and for Maryville. Much is in the balance just now – the new building may be built elsewhere...We MAY move – may MOVE – MAY MOVE – but it is all just MAYBE – so the dormitory wing construction has been postponed. At Easter I shall give you any details that are *facts*. Nothing is settled – all is unsettled now.[31]

Less than a month later, Louise received the news that Margaret Byrne had been named superior of the new Cenacle Retreat House in Metairie, Louisiana, and, though personal letters during Lent were normally not written, she wrote on March 6:

My dearest Meg,

Yes your letter certainly merits an answer even during Lent. It did not surprise me greatly but it made me very happy and at the same time very sorry for you – sorry and glad, such

---

[31] A dormitory for 200 students had been planned at the old Maryville campus, ground was broken for it on October 9, 1957, and a capital campaign for $850,000 was under way, but by early February, 1958, discussion had shifted to a move to a new campus in west Saint Louis County. The idea was strongly supported by Archbishop Ritter, who was of the opinion that the new location should be west of Lindbergh Blvd. The decision to move the campus was made in the following months.

a very strange combination. There is a parallel in the life of Blessed Philippine (in the last chapter, p. 667, if you want to check it) when Mother Boilvin,[32] her beloved old child of Florissant, writes to tell her she was to be superior at the new house in McSherrystown, Pa. Philippine answered in a hurry and I can quote her exactly in part: "After all, the blow that has struck you *God willed.* His Will is expressed by the orders of superiors." And again, "Your natural inclination is thwarted, and this shows that on your side there was nothing done even to suggest the promotion by which you – and *such a little person* you are – now find yourself superior…you must, then, bend your shoulders under the yoke…If humility is always desirable, *generous* humility is still more so." She has a good deal more to say which you might read…..I love to find faint parallels in her life. I had a great compliment at the time of Mother Shaw's death. Someone called me "her Regis Hamilton."[33] Of course it was far-fetched but I thanked Our Lord for it….

There is nothing <u>decided</u> about the moving of Maryville. The news got out in spite of us – so we had to go along with it. The new property is a few minutes (maybe a mile or so) beyond V.D. [Villa Duchesne]. The *back* entrance would be

---

[32] Julie Adeline Gonzague Boilvin, RSCJ, born 1813 in Saint Louis, entered the Society at Florissant in 1828 and was professed there in 1838. She was later superior in New York, McSherrystown, and Philadelphia. She died in 1848 at Saint-Vincent, Canada, where she had gone for a rest because of her failing health. She was one of Philippine's most beloved novices. Several of Philippine's letters to her are extant.

[33] Eulalie (Regis) Hamilton was born in Sainte Genevieve, Missouri in 1805. She was a boarding student at Florissant, where she entered the Society at age sixteen in 1821, taking the name Regis, along with her sister Mathilde Xavier (born 1802), who died soon after, in 1827. Regis was professed at Florissant in 1826. She was mistress general there in 1835, assistant superior at City House, superior at Saint Charles, then in 1847 at Saint-Jacques in Canada, Eden Hall, and Detroit, before returning to Saint Charles as superior in 1851, a year before Philippine's death in 1852, by express request of Philippine to have her back. In 1865 she went to Chicago, where she died in 1888.

on Conway, which V.D. faces. The front would be on Daniel Boone Highway. So you see it is close to the Cenacle. All depends on the sale of Maryville. We can not leave here unless we sell the place – and that is a <u>big</u> problem....[34]

You will let me know when you are coming this May, won't you? I shall get permission to go to V.D. Can a Mother Superior visit me on so special an occasion? And is the old meeting place on the roadside beneath your dignity?!

I give you no advice, my dear. I only *pray* that God will keep you well and make you aware of His Hand upon your head, His grace in your heart and will, His light in your mind. He is Love! You must be Love – You will love and so be loved. Gentle but firm – the old *fortiter suaviterque disponens omnia.*[35] My love and prayers are always with you.

Your devoted old Mother in C.J.M.,

Louise Callan r.s.c.j.

P.S. I forgot to say everyone is being nice about the book (except one Monsignor, who called it "a hunk of stuff"!) The book has already made expenses for Newman Press so that worry is off my mind. Pray that it does *real* good. Watch *America* for Father Bannon's review, and Father Bayard's (C.M.) in the *Catholic Historical Review* for April.

A few months later, on June 13, it was time for summer school:

Here we are on the verge of an invasion, of course. About thirty youngsters – asps [aspirants] and y.p's [religious in the first ten years of final profession] come in to register for summer school this afternoon. They arrive from Clifton, Coteau and the Rosary this morning, and from Villa Duchesne, St. Charles, and City House this afternoon. I have taken back the organ for

---

[34] The property of the old Maryville campus on Meramec Street in South Saint Louis was purchased by the Augustinians, who opened Augustinian Academy there in 1961. The school closed in 1972.

[35] "Strongly and gently ordering all things" (Wisd 8:1), said of Wisdom; included in the first O Antiphon of the Christmas novena.

the summer as Harriet Padberg[36] is going to Pius X for music courses – which means more queer noise in the chapel next year!....I am going to the University for a history course, U.S. since 1917 – but just to audit, 8-9:30 five days a week for six weeks, and I am teaching a course in Church History in our own summer school, 10:30-11:45. If it gets too strenuous I shall stop the university course. I am very well, as you know.

The next spring, there were more health worries. She wrote on April 12, 1959:

Dearest Meg,

Your letter gave me great joy and I am answering quickly for several reasons: 1) I have time; 2) I may not have time again soon; 3) I want to and of course I *always* do what I want to – like going to the hospital tomorrow! Dr. Gafney has me in his clutches on a new sore he wants to investigate. He says I am the most original patient he has, for I do produce the "darn'dest things." Now it's an ulcer, he thinks – but he'd like the laboratory to take a look at it. So he's going to filch it from me on Tuesday morning and I'll be at St. John's just a week – and won't my six classes have fun!? Now, Meg, I'm telling you this because I am a woman of my word of honor! I am not sick (yet) – the pain is not bad (now) – I can sit down (at present) but I expect to grow taller standing up for many a day to come!....

My book is about sold out – and Newman Press will not reprint! We can do nothing about it – but you can sell your extra copies at a high price some day!

---

[36] Harriet Ann Padberg, born in Saint Louis in 1922, entered the Society in 1943 and was professed in 1951. She was Professor of Mathematics and Music at Maryville from 1955 to 1992, and founder of the college's Department of Music Therapy in 1981. She died at Oakwood in 2014.

By June, summer life was going on as usual, while building had begun for the new Maryville. On June 12, 1959:

> Here we had the Commencement Exercises on the Feast of the Sacred Heart. It just had to be that way, according to the Archbishop's desire. It was the most crowded day imaginable. The Honors Convocation was the afternoon before, followed by High Mass at 5 P.M. and the Baccalaureate Sermon and tea. Then on the feast itself, Mass of Renovation of Vows at 7.15 (with spies in the third tribune...), examinations in Sacred Doctrine all morning, High Mass for students, parents and friends, at 11.40; buffet lunch whenever you can get it; Office, of course – (and how we miss the Grand Office, now that there is no octave); Exposition; Solemn Benediction at 4, followed by Commencement Exercises, and hospitality... and at 6.30 community feast dinner. What a day!
>
> This week we have been house-cleaning, each in her own domain. Monday we begin summer school. I am going to the University to audit a course, as I told you, then get home to teach at 10.25. We shall have about 20 of the young nuns here and not very many secular students – about ten or twelve residents on the fourth floor (always a risk in the summer!). We are supposed to have a cool summer – but the rain is harder than the heat in some ways....
>
> And how am I? If I cannot say I'M FINE, what shall I say? Dear Reverend Mother, I am in excellent condition, I am very well, I take no medicine a-tall – just vitamins; blood-count normal; heart condition excellent for an old lady; appetite normal. What more shall I say?

By November, Louise's state of health was not so bright. Explaining her long silence without a letter:

> Meg dear, there's nothing wrong except old age! I just don't make ends meet any more. It's silly, I know – but it's a fact. The college work is heavy but not more than formerly – I give too

much written work, I know. Then I get swarms of conscience that make me correct every mistake. And I fall asleep easily! As you know, I used to get an enormous amount done at night – but not now!.... I'm writing this in bed, Meg – to be honest. I have the most annoying little heart problem – not serious – no one ever dies of it – but it whips me. I've had it for years, but it has been more "active" recently – and when it goes to 135-140 for 10 hrs, I'm done for. But it doesn't happen often, I assure you, and Dr. Missey is very casual about it – so what?!

The new foundation in Houston was in preparation:

They say we are greatly needed. I guess I won't go – there is no Ph.D. in history yet ready to take my job here. But I'd make a good portress, I'm sure! And I could play the harmonium!

By February 14, 1960, she was under doctor's orders to rest, but was also beginning the abridged biography of Philippine that would appear in 1965.

I do not know why I have gotten so slowed up lately. I am very well – but I just do not get the classwork done as briskly as I used to. It may be a psychological thing – I feel so in need of preparation – even of the things I have taught for twenty years here at Maryville. Then, too, I am slower and I lose a lot of time over an order from Dr. Missey to rest awhile "supine" each day. Reverend Mother Lamy[37] thinks I'm obliged to obey it, if possible – and when I do, I'm liable to fall asleep. Woe is

---

[37] Lucy Caroline Lamy was born in Sedalia, Missouri in 1903. She graduated from Maryville College in 1925 and entered the Society in 1926 at Kenwood. After first vows in 1929, she served at City House and Villa Duchesne in Saint Louis before final profession in Rome in 1935. As treasurer or superior, she served in every house of the former Saint Louis Vicariate. In 1982 she moved to Duchesne Academy, Houston, where she died in 1997.

me! Philippine wanted no "napping old age" – but she's wished it on me.

It has been suggested that I do a shortened version of her life – to be ready for the canonization when it comes. Reverend Mother McCabe is in favor – so I am going to write to Mr. McHale of the Newman Press for *permission* to abridge my own book! I had hoped to work on a short life of Mother Lucille Mathevon this summer – but I am needed again for a summer school class. "Why certainly," says I, somewhat grudgingly inside!

May 25, Feast of Saint Madeleine Sophie, was celebrated at Maryville rather breathlessly.

We are celebrating our Mother Foundress' feast with the most crowded schedule ever concocted. Besides that "as usual" from 5^{30} to 8^{30} A.M., there is 9 Exams. 11^{40}-1^{00} as usual (P.M.) 1 Exams. 3^{00} Benediction, sermon, reception into sodality and League Promoters, 3^{30} Field-day games (relays in lounge as it is raining), 5 High Mass + Office, 6^{30} supper. 7 Class Day Exercises. 8^{30} May Procession and Crowning by candlelight. Night Prayers some time before 10 P.M.! Of course we can draw breath tomorrow and hope for fair weather....

I shall not be teaching this summer because I am going to make an abridgement of my book on Philippine to have ready for the canonization which "they say" is liable to occur in 1961. A "pretty sure" miracle is under consideration. Did I tell you they had a "Rassemblement Mondiale" of pupils of the Sacred Heart in Rome this month? 2,500 + – It must have been *some assembly*! Even the Holy Father was impressed by the 2,500 + in black dresses + veils (+ _white gloves!_) before him in St. Peter's. He showed his feelings audibly!

I must stop. It is already Thursday.[38] Pray for me. I am very well.

---

[38] May 25, 1960, was a Wednesday. This means that she was up after midnight writing.

By this time there seems to have been a schedule for this correspondence between Louise and Margaret Byrne, at twice a year, though sometimes there were more frequent letters. In her next letter, June 13, 1960, she says "Really I am improving – to think of my being on time twice in succession with my letters! I must be going 'to die or something,' as the college girls say." This time she is not teaching summer school and hopes to get out to see the new Maryville campus, where she has not been since Christmas. She is preparing for the next year's courses and is searching for suitable textbooks: "The Historical Development of Doctrine and Devotion in the Church," Church History with 65 students in two sections, as well as a course on "Causes and Leaders of the Civil War" – "fascinating, yes, but find the text book!" There is also to be a full semester symposium on Devotion to the Sacred Heart. Beyond all this, her health problems continue.

Then in my free time (9 to 11^{30} each morning, I plan), I shall work on the abridgment of Philippine. It is like cutting out vital parts of my soul. I am such a nut - and yesterday I found, in the old St. Michael's archives housed here, an *original* Duchesne letter and one of St. Madeleine Sophie. Really, God is so good to me.

He is good, Meg, in *all* He sends. You ask about me and it and the X-ray. I took seven treatments (12 min. each) and the skin would not stand any more – it cracked and misbehaved. Dr. Gafney seems to think that was enough. I do not have to go back until later, in July. I am all right, the pain is not much worse, except in bad damp weather – which is here at present. All I do out of common life is go to bed early – because I am so slow and because lying flat against the bed or pillow eases the pains, I have gained 10 pounds this year! Nothing wrong except the little lumps that develop and may be "live cancer cells wrapped in scar tissue" – and when one of them gets sore and has little knife stabs, I tell Dr. Gafney – that is, if it's bad. I can work plenty and I try to pray as much as I can while I work and when I'm not working, too! Be at peace about me. *I am fine.* I'd tell you the truth.

The next month, she wrote again, this time from Saint Charles, where she had participated in the community retreat and stayed behind some days for a rest.

> I liked the retreat very much – it was given by a Father Weber, SJ. from Denver. He had no personality but he had *God* and the things of the spirit. He stayed close to the Exercises of St. Ignatius, which I always want a retreat master to do – but he gave no stereotyped points – he had thoughts of his own – fresh, plain, simple – my style and he gave us *time for prayer*, never talking more than 30 min., often just 20 – and he remained in the chapel at his prie-dieu for the rest of the hour every meditation. The conferences were strong – no rambling stories or personal experiences – but the deep, basic things of religious life.

The new foundation of Duchesne Academy in Houston, Texas, had just been made, and her characteristic generosity made her still wonder if there was something she could do there.

> I am not equipped to teach in Texas at all. I lack physical ed. credits and 12 credits in modern methods, also credits in counselling and guidance, and the history of Texas! But they accepted an article I wrote for the Texas newspaper + N.Y. *Times* copied it. So maybe I can help remotely! But I can't teach anywhere but in college! I am *very* well, Meg – everyone tells me I look so much better since I had this wonderful holiday at St. Charles. There is no evidence, as far as I can judge, of need for more X-ray. And if there is, Meg, He can have that too. Shall I be held by threads, after cutting the ropes?

Then she reveals that her supposed holiday in Saint Charles was really editing time:

> Now Mr. John McHale of Newman Press is on the trail and there are books from him at Maryville by now – I had a kind

letter from him. But he won't republish my big *Philippine* – and the cutting is like surgery without anesthetic! I have cut 4 more chapters out here and will type them up when I go back to Maryville on Tuesday. I mean *begin* to do so. Typing is my worst enemy and penance! Excellent way to win souls for Christ. Maybe when you come home in October you can read the new manuscript! *Maybe.*

On Christmas Day, 1960:

I am better – without fever for 48 hours – after 4 weeks of just a little each day as a result of an infection in my throat. The poor old voice went out completely for a week – and I've been leading a "semi-invalid" life, when not entirely under the covers. Now I am "OK" again – a bit tired – being *careful* – and cared for more than I like to accept. *Old*, that's all!

A brief letter to another recipient tells us of her continuing interest in Philippine and the possibility of her canonization. Lucie Huger, a longtime friend of the Society in Saint Louis, was going to Rome with her husband, Bernard, at the time attorney for the Archdiocese of Saint Louis. On December 29, she writes to acknowledge Lucie's Christmas card and to ask her as she travels to Rome with the cardinal elect of Saint Louis, Archbishop Joseph Ritter, to visit the motherhouse and to ask the new cardinal to ask the pope for the canonization of Philippine: "My dear Lucie, *now* is the time, and *this* is the opportunity….Don't let us down, Lucie – we count on *YOU*."[39]

---

[39] In a follow up conversation in 1997 with Lucie Huger, Mary Gray McNally, RSCJ, learned that Lucie took the request very seriously and herself wrote a letter to the pope, via her husband and the Vatican Secretary of State. She later received an acknowledgement that the pope had seen it. Lucie Furstenberg Huger was a Villa Duchesne and Maryville graduate. She died in 2005. Mary Gray McNally (1912-2005) was mistress general and superior in several houses of the Saint Louis Province. At the time of Louise's death in 1966, she was president of Maryville College.

TO THE NEW
MARYVILLE CAMPUS

Her health problems did not keep her from welcome travel. On April 4, 1961, she writes from Newton College of the Sacred Heart in Boston, attending with Mother Patricia Barrett meetings of the Society of College Teachers of Sacred Doctrine. With talks by Gustave Weigel, S.J., and Barnabas Ahern, C.P., and a broadly ecumenical content, she relished the program. But the move to the new Maryville campus had begun:

> We have begun to move. Four of the nuns are living out at the new place, as of yesterday. Address: 13350[40] Conway Road, St. Louis 41 after mid-May. I may go out sooner. Will let you know. Any suggestions for a course in Old Testament? I'm in for that for 1st sem. 1961-62; New Test. 2nd sem. with freshman division. Love and close union of prayer in C.J.M.

By Pentecost Sunday, 1961, Louise had moved to the new campus. Her detailed description is an important piece of collective memory of the campus as it was seen then, so different from today, and of the adventures of living in a construction zone.

> You see I am one of the "foundresses" out here on the new frontier! Mothers Adams and Scott, Sisters Hines and

---

[40] The address was actually 13550 Conway Road.

Murphy[41] came out early in April when this building was turned over to us more or less completed. I came out the first week of May after my classes were accelerated to a finish and ready for examinations – the Commencement took place on May 19. The first Mass was offered on May 2nd, with the Senior Class present. It was followed by their farewell dinner – a box supper, this time, on the east terrace of the administration building. Since then we have had Mass daily. The Benedictines from the Saint Louis Priory School are chaplains – now the Father Prior and now the Father Treasurer. I have the honor of being sacristan pro tem – and it is tremendous joy. I am also first, second, and third portress and receptionist and Madame du Tour![42] I have shown the place to so many groups – ten or twelve some days, and a wheel-chair guest yesterday – I feel like a little broken record, or a disc on a telephone!

Some day when you come again to visit us, you will see it all. It is in a most beautiful setting – and it is all very dignified and functional – and the old parlor furnishings from Maryville South have been refinished beautifully and look quite warm and homelike in their new abode. Everyone thinks the decorators did a good job. The dominant color inside and out

---

[41] Eleanor Adams, RSCJ, born in Troy, Missouri, in 1918, entered the Society in 1947, was professed in 1956, and served in most of the houses of the Saint Louis Vicariate in many different offices, including superior. At the time of the campus move, she was treasurer at Maryville. She died in Saint Charles in 2007. Mary Louise Scott, RSCJ, was born in Saint Louis in 1906, entered in 1931, was professed in 1939, and served in many houses of the vicariate. She was for many years dean of students at Maryville, and in 1961 worked in development for the college. Geraldine Hines, RSCJ, born in 1899, entered in 1919 and was professed in 1928, all in Saint Louis. She died in Saint Charles in 1965. Gertrude Leona Murphy, RSCJ, was born in Alma, Arizona in 1893, entered at Grand Coteau in 1925, and was professed in New Orleans in 1934. She died in 1973 in Saint Charles.

[42] The reference is to Hélène du Tour, RSCJ (1787-1849 or 1850), early missionary to America in 1827, who died at Natchitoches, Louisiana. Louise knew of her as a contemporary of Philippine on the frontier, but here is using her name as a play on words.

is green – nature and grace working together. The entire top floor of the administration building is the cloistered convent. Offices and parlors occupy the first floor (front level). The temporary chapel is also on that floor, right wing in the picture. This will eventually be part of the library; at present the library is below the chapel on the ground floor – you can see we have three complete stories (storeys?) but only two open on the front level. The ground floor also contains the students' dining room in the east wing (library is west wing), the serving rooms, kitchens etc., small dining rooms for priests, guests, Sisters of Notre Dame de Sion who are studying in the college (we had 7 this year, from Kansas City), Community refectory, etc., etc., and the boiler room.

Much of the building was still in process, and not always successful process.

The classroom buildings – 1. Liberal Arts and 2. Science, are to the west behind the library-chapel wing. These are ready to be occupied. On the east beyond the cafeteria wing and facing the classroom buildings the dormitory buildings are rising rather slowly, but promised for occupancy by the end of September – we open in Oct. These buildings are not shown in the little sketch, but they stand on the east and west of the "Mall" – as the expanse of ground behind the administration building is termed in the architect's drawings. The concrete walks over this area have been laid and the landscapers have done a great deal in the way of leveling, planting grass, strewing gravel (which they call *chat*) and getting things in fair shape. The weather has been torrential, so we have some red clay lakes where the excavations for the service road were under way. We have also a few hundred leaks which let in floods during the worst storm – a blessing from heaven – the *damage* was not great but the defects in construction were magnificently exposed – before the community moved in. Now all is being remedied – we hope.

The move was well organized but some found the new arrangements a difficult adjustment.

The moving has been something to read about. A good friend, Mr. B. Kearns, and his brother Jo – both married to Maryville alumnae, undertook the "minor moving" for us, free cost! Trucks and vans paid for by themselves or borrowed by them for five or six successive Saturdays – making as many as nine trips each Saturday. Five hundred student chairs came yesterday and were placed properly at once, plus all the students' dining room furniture – fifty tables and about four hundred chairs – also the students' lounge and snack shop tables and chairs. The Saturday before that, 40,000 library books came in Budweiser boxes – a conveyor belt set up at rear entrance of Old M. shot the boxes down the back outside steps to trucks, and another out here set up at library entrance shot the boxes in to the New M. library – all so marked as to be identified as to contents and then stacked in order. When the new shelving and equipment comes, it will not be too hard to put the 40,000 books in place….It will be more difficult to make the new place home to some of the older nuns, I fear. Even the hot and cold water faucets are queer new gadgets….

Now I must stop and take a turn at the door. No cubby holes in this building – but "offices" in classroom buildings. We shall all need raincoats and rain hoods for the trek to classes…. You know what a foundation means. So far no mice in *this* building! But lovely little birds killing themselves by dashing against the great expanses of glass!

On July 30 she wrote again, saying that all the moving was now done, though the 40,000 books had not yet been unpacked. There was no call bell system, as was the case in other convents, "but a P.A. system that echoes names all over the place and there is no hushing it up unless you answer. But it is all a great adventure and I have had the audacity to gain six pounds amidst the most exercise I have EVER taken in all my life." She is delighted to have a garden with blue urns and rose petunias, and there are blackberries to harvest in the woods, where there are "no snakes or chiggers to bother us. You may not believe me, but we have very few mosquitoes [on the third floor where the convent is] because they do not fly this high! But small toads leap up to second story galleries!"

Administration Building
Maryville College of the Sacred Heart
13550 Conway, Route #1, Box 94
St. Louis 41, Missouri

Notecard of Gander Hall Administration building at the new Maryville in west Saint Louis County, 1961

At Thanksgiving, she bemoans her weight gain:

I am very well – getting too heavy for comfort in my clothes…but all this is rather concealed from the general public, so the last eight or ten pounds are not too evident. I must blame all this on the "country air" – for I certainly take more exercise than I have done for YEARS. I go out, of course, six or eight times a day – and the Liberal Arts building where I teach is quite a step away. It takes me about eight minutes to go from my own sleeping room (I hate the word <u>cell</u>) to the classroom on the other side of the "mall" – as they call the central elipse (ellipse?) around which the buildings are erected. The plan certainly is good – but time consuming.

Louise was now given a new project. She was asked by Reverend Mother Vicar Angela McCabe to bring *The Society of the Sacred Heart in North America* up to date to 1965, the centenary of the death of Saint Madeleine Sophie. In preparation for this task, she wrote to various houses, gathered notes, and visited them when possible, especially those founded after 1937, the cutoff date of the first edition. It was a project that she was never able to complete, even though she was eventually given some relief from teaching in order to work on it. From this point on, the revision of the book was a topic often commented upon, along with her continuing health problems. Eventually, her decline in health slowed and then stopped the momentum of the revision of the book.

Also I meant to tell you a parable from nature. I watch the sunrise sometimes during my meditation, for I have an east cell. There is no really great beauty at sunrise unless there are *clouds* – they are the material on which the sun's light plays its effects. So clouds in our life – not the heavy black kind – but all the things that darken the horizon of the soul at times. The *Light* plays His effects in the soul – now just marvel at how *deep* I'm becoming!

The first Christmas in the new buildings was troubled for Louise because she had not received the usual letter from Margaret Byrne. "Will someone of the Cenacle community let me know if you are ill, or gone to Australia, or fallen in the lake?" Nevertheless, the holiday was "a quiet, happy Christmas in our new home. The chapel is rather woodsy with evergreen trees." Eighty-five trees had been planted, walkways were being constructed, and the two dormitories were finished. A chaplain's house for Msgr. James Curtin, archdiocesan superintendent of schools, was in construction; once moved in, he would occupy it for many years with his Dachshund Buster, who was often loaned to Louise for walks. Both priest and dog became fast friends of Louise and of Sister Marie, a close friend in community who was devoted to Louise.[43] With Msgr. Curtin's help, Louise established a magnificent rose garden in back of the administration building that was known to be her work and for which she was responsible for many years. As she gardened, she was able to strike up conversations with passersby that became an important outreach. She wrote later that she would spend three or four hours a day during the summer on the garden, and had the satisfaction of seeing some of the roses on the altar each morning, and providing fresh flowers for the superior to take to sick nuns. "It is a rewarding job, this gardening, and it keeps me very well" (letter of August 15, 1963).

Msgr. James Curtin (1914-1977), longtime resident at Maryville
Photo courtesy of the St. Louis Archdiocesan Archives

---

[43] Marie Christine Schlosser, RSCJ, was born in 1892 in Cincinnati, where she entered the novitiate in 1916. She came to Maryville in 1919, made her profession there in 1925, and never left, except with the community to the new Maryville in 1961, until she moved to Regis community in Saint Charles in 1972. She died there Nov. 30, 1976.

Louise Callan, Sister Marie Schlosser, and
Buster sometime after 1961

On February 7, 1962:

We have had a pretty cold winter with lots of snow – and there is more to come, I am sure. But we are not snowbound – classes go on and the nuns all go out from one building to another as if we had been doing it always. I have a fine rain cape and hood in which I array myself…. I am doing a course in Devotion to the Sacred Heart again, with about 25 seniors – it is wonderful how much they get out of it. Of course the textbook *Heart of the Saviour* by Stierli, S.J.[44] is a real challenge, which is an excellent thing. We are having a CCD training course also this semester. I am eager to audit that.

In 1962, the correspondence with Margaret Byrne becomes more frequent. At Easter Louise refers to the "upsurge of prejudice and pride in N.O. It is terrible at a distance – so I can imagine how it is right on the spot." She is still energetic about travel and uses this as proof that she is well.

---

[44] Josef Stierli, S.J., ed., *Heart of the Saviour: A Symposium on Devotion to the Sacred Heart.* Freiburg: Herder, 1958.

I am going to Detroit this afternoon with Mothers Keyes and Barrett for the meetings of the Society of Catholic College Teachers of Sacred Doctrine. You should belong to it. I'll also lecture at Grosse Pointe [a school in the Detroit area], visit the new place we built outside Detroit at Bloomfield Hills, and go over to Buffalo to see our new convent there. Now all this tells you I am *very* well, doesn't it?

Another letter at Pentecost, June 10, reports on the successful trip, including that "the flight back over the lake [Lake Michigan] was lovely, perfect flying weather. We had come up from Saint Louis on a jet in gray fog and clouds all the way! I thought jets got above such things as earthy fog." Msgr. Curtin had now moved into his house on the campus and would also teach Dogmatic Theology in the college and say a daily Mass for the students on campus. "We had to build him a residence – and I think we won his heart by consulting him about the plans and letting him suggest – and then accepting his suggestions. He seems very much at home with us and I believe we can have a most helpful and kind friend." Finally for the summer of 1962, she has no teaching responsibilities so that she can devote all her time to the revision of *The Society of the Sacred Heart in North America* for 1965. The project also occupied the majority of her time in the summer of 1963.

On August 27, she writes again, deploring again the situation of racial tension in New Orleans:

> I get so distressed when I think of Christians being so un-Christian, Catholics being so un-Catholic. What a dreadful thing prejudice is! I am impressed, in what I read about the preparations for the Ecumenical Council, at the honest way the Church is facing up to Catholic prejudice and trying to overcome it on all levels.

About this time, the first black students attended Maryville and received a warm welcome from Louise. The following incident was witnessed by one who remembered it. A Maryville student from New

Orleans whose mother had attended the Rosary said to Louise: "My mother says it's just terrible we are taking blacks." With her typical verve, Louise responded: "I taught your mother, you know, dear. Will you go home and tell your mother that I know the blood lines of every family in that school."

In the same letter of August 27, she notes her continued travel, not only to the Washington meeting of the Catholic Sociological and Political Science Associations, but to the Sacred Heart houses in New York and Portsmouth, Rhode Island. These school visits were for the purpose of the updated history project. Her goal for this project is still 1965 at this time.

The frequency of the correspondence continues unabated in 1962 and 1963. So does the travel. On October 7, she writes of plans to go south to give several talks and do research for the revised history project until the 15th. But on October 22, she writes to modify the plan: by railroad on November 8 to New Orleans to speak there to a "mixed group" on November 9, then fly to Houston on Monday, November 12, to speak to the students, then return to New Orleans to take a 4:30 p.m. train back to Saint Louis, arriving the morning of November 13. In a short note on December 1 she comments: "Since we returned from N.O. I have just about 'met myself in reverse,' trying to catch up with my work—plus some gardening, of course." On New Year's Eve, she is on the train returning from professional meetings in Chicago, "making our day of recollection in part on the train."[45]

By February 17, 1963, she has missed the last two weeks of the first semester ("but I was up for the examinations!") and first two weeks of the second semester through unspecified illness. Her classwork has been reduced, however, and she looks forward to spending more time on the new edition of the history during Lent and the summer. Her gardening continues, aided continually by gifts of roses from Msgr. Curtin, at one time called "Msgr. Curtin of the Roses." On April 21:

---

[45] One of Louise's brothers had a high position in the Illinois Central Railroad, the line that ran from Chicago to Saint Louis to New Orleans. She was able to get free passes for any of the nuns when they traveled this route, and frequently used it herself.

Dearest Meg,

You are worrying at my silence – I have to scribble this because one finger of the right hand is in a splint – freak accident to the extensor tendon ("caught the baseball the wrong way," Dr. Roche said). Nothing serious, just awkward. I was *so* glad to have your Easter letter. I am very well – no leftovers from the virus – except a cough that stirs itself up at unexpected times.

In spite of the virus I have some gardens planted – and a bed of roses from Msgr. Curtin.

I went to hear Father Hans Kung at the close of the NCEA. He is really terrific. My reaction is this: Our Lord in the sermon on the mount said to the Jews "Bring yourselves up to date!" "It was said *of old,*…but I say…." That is what the Holy Father and Fr. Rahner and Fr. Kung and others are saying – I'm glad I'm alive.

On May 24th:

Here we are on the eve of our feasts [St. Madeleine Sophie May 25, Our Lady of the Cenacle May 31] – This will show you where my thoughts and prayers are. I am really slowed up, otherwise once in a while I'd catch up on letters and be on time…. The school year is almost over – one more week of exams. We have had strangely chilly and wet weather for two weeks – bad on gardens and also on garden parties – but the cool weather is helpful for the exams. My summer will be gardening, trying to help a young nun with a history thesis, trying, too, to get on with bringing the *Society of the S. H. in N.A.* up to date and my spiritual life up to the level He expects. I did so want to go to a Scripture institute in Detroit on *Teaching O.T. in college* – but it was not approved. I can, of course, go on teaching myself!

On August 15, she has just emerged from the annual community retreat, with which she was not happy.

We came out of retreat this morning – a retreat given by Father McGinnis, head of the Theology Department, Regis College, Denver. He is a bull-dog looking Jesuit and his retreat manner is "not too attractive" to a person like me who shudders at shouting in the chapel and loathes modern jargon. I was in awe and wonder constantly at the vocabulary he managed to use with apparently no effort. I had a hard time translating "the posture of my conscious before principiative knowledge," "the sophistication of integral Christians before the cultural exigencies of their historic milieu," "the fringe aspects of being involved in the apostolic process," and "the whole series of polarities arising from the historical context in function of emitting religious vows." Now I ask you…But the key question is this: "What is the moral posture with which I confront the things that challenge me?" – and this, especially, in the apostolic venture? Try this out on your community and you may acquire vast "insights" on the "personal dimensions" of each one! "Dimension" was a pet word with Father McGinnis, and every time he used it I thought of how much more I weigh now than at old Maryville, or how much wider the girth is!!!

You are right in your conclusion – I did not like the retreat – but I stuck to it, with the help of an excellent book, the French Jesuit Longhaye's *Retraite Annuelle de Huit Jours*. It is an old friend – often my refuge….

After giving news of the college and her courses for the fall, she returns tongue in cheek to the retreat:

I meant to ask you whether you understand the lapidary quality of the ideal posited in each of the beatitudes – and whether you realize that the second part of each beatitude is the psychological posture of one who has the lapidary quality expressed in the first part…Now this might make a very engrossing subject for spiritual conversation at the New Orleans Cenacle some evening when the community is in need of real relaxation after a challenging high school retreat…or an integrated one.

On September 22:

> We have a good enrollment – about 50 more than last year. There is talk of more buildings – fine arts and a chapel. The new tennis courts are a fine addition. We have 212 acres now and about 3½ miles of trail on the property for horseback riding.
>
> Yes, Meg, the decades certainly are mounting – 24th year straight! [at Maryville] And things are so different now. The Bible course is my joy (and distress at times) – I have 2 sections this year, about 40 minutes each….I'm trying to write this against the noise of a "Hootenanny" the students are having – harmless but harrowing!

A quick note on November 29 reveals new health problems.

Dearest Meg,

> It was so good to hear from you – and oh! Thank God our national tragedy [the assassination of President John F. Kennedy on November 22] did not happen in New Orleans…. Meg, I am at St. John's Hospital. I was catapulted here Wednesday. I'm not sick – but a problem has developed. Because I have been getting so short of breath and had several long rapid-heart spells, I went to see Dr. Missey Monday. He sent me to X-ray for a chest plate, which revealed a quantity of fluid in the right lung. As soon as he read the film he phoned at one o'clock for me to be at the hospital by 3:30. By 5 o'clock two doctors had punctured me and suctioned off about a quart of fluid. Then I could breathe normally, tho' there is much more to come out. Now the question is: what will the laboratory find? Live cancer cells? Dr. Gafney is on the case, of course. If he has to operate, I'll let you know. I am very well, otherwise – have not lost weight (140 lbs!) – have not much pain. I am distressed about my five classes but am trying to plan for them – just 2 ½ weeks, to Dec. 18 – but they had lost so much as a result of the tragedy, plus Thanksgiving.

Msgr. Curtin gave me a dozen more rosebushes, which I had just got into the ground when I had to pack a few things in a bag and take off.

Louise was in the hospital for nearly two weeks, where a malignancy was discovered in her lung. She wrote from there on December 8, her 70th birthday:

Dearest Meg,

How grateful I am to you for the phone call and the birthday letter and picture and the prayers and the love behind it all! This is a strange sort of birthday. Low Mass in the hospital chapel. I sang the *Gaudens Gaudebo* [opening words of the liturgy of the Immaculate Conception] in my heart, knowing the *Liber*[46] melodies so well. I shall not sing much more aloud. It requires too much breath and there is pain. The pain is going to be there, so I must learn to live with it more than ever. But as far as medical science is concerned, all is under control for the moment. The malignancy is in the lining of the lung and may be of *very* slow growth – but will call for treatment – how often I don't know.

Now Meg, "Jesus tacebat" [Matt 26:63] He didn't say much about all the suffering that was ahead of Him – and yet, when it was upon Him, He admitted it so simply. That's all.

Dr. Gaffney says I can go home to Maryville tomorrow – I can go on with my class work. I am no invalid, but I need to be a little careful – no lifting heavy things – no *strenuous* digging in the rose bed! Some extra rest – (It's *snowing*!!!)

Beg your nuns to keep me in their prayers more than ever and give them so much love. Take care of my Meg. You know the love of

Yours devotedly in C.J.M.

---

[46] The *Liber Usualis*, the standard book of liturgical chant in use in the Latin liturgy.

Soon after Christmas, on December 28, she writes from home that she should have written sooner but has been busy helping the superior, Reverend Mother Stanley,[47] with thank you notes for Christmas gifts to the community.

Now that excuse should make you realize I am no invalid! I'm really better. Of course, "it did get me, but it didn't get me down" – that's a very frivolous slogan, but it's a good one for the motivation is from His Heart.

She was able to attend the Christmas midnight Mass and one in the morning, and get to the refectory for breakfast and dinner Christmas day "and the same since. We do not know what the early January chest plate will show but I hope to get back to the classroom." She was still in charge of the grounds and because of milder weather, has gotten out to see about tree and rose planting. "I won't be able to *dig* as I did last summer, but I can supervise!"

But still, I'm doing very nicely, thank you! Dr. Missey says I have blood that will fight anything – and I am determined to cooperate with him and Dr. Gafney and Reverend Mother and Sister Richard,[48] our infirmarian. So much about myself! But I want you to know how much we have to be thankful for. Meg, if this is *His test* of my sincerity in consecration to His Heart and His Will, I do want to get A+ in faith and trust and love…. Early in January I'll go over to the new St. John's just 5 minutes up Conway Road from here, as an outpatient for tests and chest plate. That needs prayers, so beg your dear nuns to help me more than ever. I'm spoiled with help both natural and supernatural.

---

[47] Agnes Ruth Stanley was born in Saint Louis in 1910, entered the Society in 1933, and was professed at Kenwood in 1942. She was superior or coordinator in every house of the Saint Louis Vicariate/Province, known for her breadth of spirit during times of difficult transitions. She died at Oakwood in 2003.

[48] Effie Richard, RSCJ, was born in 1897 in Youngstown, Louisiana, entered in 1921 at Grand Coteau and was professed in 1932 in Saint Louis. She died in 1973 at Grand Coteau.

The early January tests were not good. Reverend Mother Ruth Stanley, RSCJ, superior at Maryville, wrote to Margaret Byrne on January 13, 1964, that the fluid had returned to Louise's lung, requiring another hospitalization until February 3.

> She may not teach at present and unless God steps in she will not teach any more. This is a tremendous sacrifice but her generosity is a constant edification to all of us. At present she is not suffering too much and the suffering is not constant. My hope is boundless. I keep thinking that Blessed Philippine will do something for our dear Mother Callan. Even if she doesn't cure her completely she might make the disease go very slowly but both Mother Callan and I are only asking for His Will in His way. Often she says to me "In His Will is my peace." This is the atmosphere of her life right now. She is as it were giving our Lord everything before He has a chance to take it.

A week after release from the hospital, on February 11, Louise wrote that she was "pretty shaken up after the very drastic treatments," but is now trying to regain her stride. Not teaching in the spring semester, she will instruct a convert entrusted to her by Msgr. Curtin. Being freed of teaching allowed her more time for her two favorite occupations, gardening and updating the Society history. On March 30, she writes that her love of flowers has produced several visitors with azalea bushes, blue phlox in full bloom, pansies, and peonies, though the weather is still so cold that some of it needs to be nurtured indoors for a while. Though she is not teaching, she has been able to maintain her spacious office with good light, a place to keep the plants alive until the weather warms up. She is also energetically back at work on the history updating.

> I am getting along with the revision of *The Society of the Sacred Heart in North America*. Some of the houses have been very co-operative, both east and west – and some are too busy to help much. However, I have a plot against them and I believe it will work. I shall write them up in brief fashion, using the vague material of the Annual Letters, then send them the sheet

or sheets for approval.... When they see themselves so briefly summed up, they will come to or come around or come across – as you choose. The Canadian houses responded so well, I have their sheets all approved and corrected by themselves. The same with Eden Hall and Overbrook in Philadelphia. Of course, our own have "done swell" – except St. Charles. It's not easy to sum up the past twenty-five years of development for any house – except for the new ones that have been opened since 1940. The Far West sent me "volumes" about themselves!!! I am going to add an entire chapter on foundations since World War II. There have been very interesting ones – San Diego, El Cajon, Miami, Houston, Princeton, Newton College, Winnipeg and Buffalo – and several transfers, like Elmhurst from Providence, R.I., to Portsmouth; Lawrence Avenue, Detroit, to Bloomfield Hills; Woodlands is the new academy in Lake Forest, transferred from Barat College to an entirely new "plant" – twelve acres cut off from the college campus by a deep ravine – and with an entirely separate community. Fortunately, I visited there, and Portsmouth, and Houston, and Buffalo, and Bloomfield Hills before I got on the sick list. I almost wish I felt sick sometime! Now isn't that an ungrateful thought??? You know what I mean.

By May 3, however, something had shifted in her attitude toward the work, even though she was not having medical complications: "I spend about two hours every morning (in the garden) and some time in the afternoon. The typewriter and I are not as frequent companions as we should be, but there is little incentive to that research project. I know – feelings don't count, but they get in the way." There is nothing in the correspondence to explain this change in motivation. Her blood count was good and she did not have to return to the hospital until June. Her next appointment would be on May 7 – "Ascension Day – but doctors do not seem to think of that on their calendar." Those who knew her lung problem marveled at how well she looked. "I fear I shall get no more cards of 'sympathy' and 'get well' and such things."

On June 9, it was time for more tests. She was proud of the fact that she had not been in the hospital since March 21, "a very fine record!

Today I go for blood tests and X-ray (chest plates) – which will tell the tale and decide my fate." That fate was to be back in the hospital June 14-20. "Don't expect me to be pale and thin and haggard! I look *very* well, even if the 'moon-face,' as the doctors call it, is the result of antibiotics." Indeed she was doing very well at this point, much better than had been expected a few months before. On July 12, she is home for "a stretch of terribly wet weather and extra humid sunny days – and this is all against me – but I get along very well, even with the pain. The gardens are about drowned – and the weeds are having a field-day – but all will be well!"

On September 2, her roses were suffering in the late summer heat, but the abridged version of her biography of Philippine Duchesne, on which she had labored for so long, was at the printer and would be out in spring of 1965. She was also going back to teaching one class in fall semester, and two were planned for the spring semester.

Sometime in the previous months, Louise's last sibling, Kathryn, had died. She wrote: "I am afraid I have let her death get under my skin a bit – I mean personally. I did not consider before it happened, what it meant to be the last of the generation. Strange how the psychological works on the physical, isn't it?" Margaret Byrne remembered an earlier episode regarding this sister. Previously at some time when Louise was in the hospital and Margaret was visiting, Kathryn appeared unannounced, having come all the way from Tennessee to see her sister. Louise refused to see her and told her to go back home, since she had no permission to see her. Margaret told her she was being rigid, which Louise first denied, then later admitted. It was a remarkable change in Louise's attitude from the free spirit of earlier days, and a contrast to the open mindedness that she often talked about.

The unexpected decline in interest in the revision project, though she did not say so in early May, may have been the constant pain with which she was now living. On October 29, she wrote: "I push the pen badly and cannot manage the typewriter with ease – just a coward about pain, that's all. So my manuscript has not advanced a page in three months, but I am well." But she clearly had not given up on the project, which she would mention again at Christmas.

The General Chapter of 1964 was underway in Rome. "What shall come out of it? More 'tailored' habits? Minor changes? All the professed religious were free to make suggestions, of course. I sent a few notes – nothing startling! We need to 'open the windows' along some lines." On Christmas Day, she writes again about two outcomes of the recent General Chapter. One of the ways of opening windows was preparation for the arrival of a number of "aspirants," young religious not finally professed, into the community for as long as three years of theological study, called Doctrinal Formation. "The adjustment will be a problem and Reverend Mother Vicar thinks I may be able to help with them." At the same time, the distinction between "choir nuns" and "coadjutrix sisters" was in its final stages of being abolished, which brought more changes to community life. "The Sisters are all very dear about it – so simple and joyous."

Margaret had recently sent Louise a card with some inspiring saying about being "unlimited." Louise replied:

> I can understand why you like it so much. Yet I would argue that word *unlimited* – for it is only so where circumstances, place and time allow. How *completely* limited I am, save in prayer. Yes, I can walk Monsignor Curtin's dog in an almost unlimited fashion and with a supernatural motive – and sort mail and attend to the switchboard and water the house plants and read! The nun's vocation – *any* nun's—is limited by the very fact that she is consecrated. But that's enough – we'll talk that over some day.
>
> I have had a tussle with Mr. McHale of Newman Press about the illustrations in the abridged edition of *Philippine*. I won, thank God – and I think I can get the revised edition of *The Society of the S.H. in N. A.* accepted more easily than I had anticipated. Herder has almost *asked* for the manuscript! But that is a year from now, at least.
>
> I saw Dr. Gafney on Dec. 22. He seemed satisfied but I *may* have to go in for treatment in January – have not had to since early June! I am not sick. I am just handicapped by loving care and scientific medication!

The hunch that she would have to return to the hospital in January proved true. On New Year's Day, 1965, she wrote: "I go to St. John's on the 3rd of Jan. for a few days' treatment. Dr. Gafney insists, in spite of the fact that all is well! My 'Amen' is not very generous, but I *mean* it with mind and will. The heart, I suppose, is out of step."

By March 2, she is again able to take up teaching in spite of what was thought the previous year, that she would no longer be able to be in the classroom. She is again in the fervor of classroom activity, with the added burden of finalizing the abridged biography:

Dearest Meg,

This is the eleventh hour, but I have been under such pressure for the past two weeks, I could do no better. I had to proof-read both sets of galleys for the new *Philippine Duchesne* by myself. [49] The page proofs went into the mail yesterday morning and the *Index* by air last night, and there were classes today and a visit in the parlor. And we are losing Mother Happy to Villa Duchesne in half an hour. How I shall miss her! She is the hardest-working religious I have *ever* known and the readiest to help anyone at any time. She has been so kind to me – as infirmarian those bad years at old Maryville, and as everything here at the new place. I had her in class in 1921-1922, when I was an aspirant [not finally professed], and we have lived together so often. The Rosary years are a precious memory on so many counts.

Apparently her teaching at this time was limited to the young religious in Doctrinal Formation, for she adds: "I am pretty well, Meg. No real complaint! But I do miss the college. Young nuns *are* nuns!"

After a silence of six months, on June 25 Louise resumes the correspondence. She has determined that the treatment in the hospital will not be repeated.

---

[49] She means the galleys and the page proofs. Before digital layout, authors were first given galleys on which the text was not yet set on pages, then later, the page proofs. Errors could occur in the transfer from galley to page proof, so both had to be carefully checked.

Dearest Meg,

How good you are to me! Such a dear letter! So many good prayers! And so much good news! I have some "Good News" roses this year. Meg, I am *all right* but my arm is like a ham and my hand like a catcher's mit [sic] most of the time and typing is a torture, but I do not forget, and I assure you Mother Happy or Mother Bascom would let you know if anything went badly. I shall never take the treatment again. I do not have to, morally. I can't endure it again physically. I am very well for one who is considered *ill*. And it is very strange that I can play the organ, as I am doing while Mother Padberg is teaching 8 weeks at Manhattanville. Some of the nuns are enjoying the old hymns that I have resurrected. The fingers work automatically. I'm trying to translate the Latin hymns – not too successful.

I have a boy who helps me in the garden. I do not do the hard work anymore – but I love to be outside – it makes breathing easier and gives an appetite!

On September 18, she writes about damage done to both New Orleans and Miami, to the Cenacle, Sacred Heart, and friends and family of both congregations by Hurricane Betsy on September 6-13. Meanwhile, she is back to teaching with three sections of "freshman Scripture," two of college students and one in "the juniorate with just ten young nuns – all very interesting."

How am I? JUST FINE….and that is true. Dr. Gafney was pleased when I was at the hospital for a check last Thursday. He thinks he will find an excuse for putting me back in the hospital – but the chest plate and blood count are OK – so….

A chatty letter at Christmas gives details of celebrations at the college which had also for some years been the location of Incarnate Word Parish as the parish built its own church. Three of the five Sunday Masses were staffed with student volunteer babysitters. Many alumnae lived locally and attended. "Of course, I have very little part in this, but

I can smile and be friendly." As harbinger of change, the City House community left cloister to attend Midnight Mass next door at the Cathedral instead of in their own convent, at the request of Cardinal Ritter. Louise was looking forward to a trip to New Orleans, returning on January 2, 1966, and had courageously relented about her decision to discontinue treatment:

> [On January 2] I go in to St. John's that afternoon for a session of treatment. I proclaimed aloud to all and sundry that I would never take the treatment again – it undid me so completely last January – but Dr. Gafney made it sound so stupid to risk losing all we have gained just through cowardice, that I asked Monsignor Curtin what he thought. He had told me I was not obliged to take it – but he said it sounded more like common sense to take no risk. So I go. Home on Jan 8 – and the second semester begins only on Jan 17, so I'll have time to recuperate! I will be teaching three courses this semester – not three sections of the same Scripture course, as last semester. I'll have one Old Testament, one New Testament (with 12 aspirants), and one history, Colonial America. It seems a long time since I taught history, though I did a tutorial with one young nun last year. I am really very well – 120 lbs.[50] – I do get tired easily, but I am getting old – and I loved your dear birthday card and note.
>
> Now I must stop – 5.10 – see how slowly I type! Keep me more than ever in your prayers. I may write from N.O. if there is opportunity. I wish you'd pray for my niece, Cecil Allen. She will never get over the fact that Sacred Heart nuns marched in Montgomery[51] – that was again the subject of her Christmas long distance.... She breaks my heart but I can not make her

---

50   She had lost 20 lbs. in the last year.

51   On March 21-25, 1965, four RSCJ joined the 3200 people who walked from Selma to Montgomery, Alabama: Sisters Patricia Barrett and Anne Webster from Maryville College, and Sisters Nancy Kane and Marguerite Green from Barat College, Lake Forest, Illinois, along with college students from both institutions.

understand. So – Changing your habit? I wonder which of us will do it first! We have no idea what is ahead, but the change is in preparation for us, too. Shall we go into designing?

A short note on February 13 reports that the New Orleans trip was a happy one. But "I had a rough time at the hospital" afterwards, then she was laid low by a terrible cold for three weeks, "doctors not withstanding!" The teaching goes smoothly, but she has difficulty when teaching Exodus to get across to students basic exegetical thinking.

That the first nine plagues are not monumental miracles seems heresy to them – as did the literary treatment of Genesis 1-11. It takes a long time to get them to accept that fact that it is not a question of "Did this really happen?" but of "What does this Mean?" Once they get that principle really made their own, things change. Perhaps I should say "Once they accept that challenge"...I marvel that they understand my old-fashioned language – but they do!

On April 17, she is back to the new habit.

We have seen a picture of the new habit. It is so plain, I marvel how anyone thought it up. Black. No cape. Not too short (4 in.) Box plaits in the skirt. Wisp of white collar. White piece across forehead and over ears to back of neck. Black veil (no doubt the one we now have). I can't say it "improves our image" but it certainly looks dead. Now, of course, it may turn out to be very practical and nice. A small picture really cannot give detail. [52]

---

[52] While change of habit for RSCJ was in the planning through much of 1966, it was implemented on January 1, 1967, several months after Louise's death.

Sister Corinne Happy in the new habit worn from January 1, 1967

On June 12, she writes from Omaha, where she has gone to attend lectures on Saint Paul by Kathryn Sullivan, RSCJ.[53] Earlier, she had made the community retreat at Maryville, not much to her liking.

> We made our retreat May 28-June 6. It was given by a young Jesuit, his first 8 day retreat. It was so new breed and off

---

[53] Kathryn Lois Sullivan, RSCJ, was born in Philadelphia in 1905. She entered the Society in 1928 and was professed in 1937. Like Louise, her doctorate from University of Pennsylvania was in American History, received before profession in 1936 because she had begun work on it before entering the Society. She was Professor of History at Manhattanville College, but because of advantageous clerical scholarly connections, she began already in the 1940s to move into the newly developing field of Scripture. By the mid-1960s, she was being called upon to lecture widely, nationally and increasingly internationally. She like Louise was held back by authority from realizing the full impact that she could have made, but Louise must have seen Kathryn as far more successful, and she was intimidated when expected to teach young religious who had already attended lectures by Kathryn at Kenwood. She died in 2006.

beat, I took to a good retreat from Reverend Mother Mulqueen's "inner closet," and had peace. I really do not see why there has to be such a complete deviation from the Exercises, why the retreat is reduced to three talks a day, at times accompanied by records with men singing homemade psalms accompanied by banjo or guitar. I know I am old fashioned, but I cannot help it!

The subject of the updated history appears once more. Her superior wanted her to resume work on it; she had set it aside because of illness in 1963. Now, publication in 1968, the sesquicentennial of Philippine's arrival, is the goal. "I am well enough, but I have rather lost interest. Maybe Philippine will help with this, too." But her roses continue to occupy her attention: "I wish you could have seen my roses the past three weeks. 64 bushes in full bloom. Just lovely! Even Monsignor Curtin was pleased. The rest of the garden is rather neglected and overgrown. I cannot do as much as formerly – old and lazy!"

The history update was never to be completed. She was probably more aware of her diminishment than she would admit to her dearly beloved Margaret. In a letter to another RSCJ on August 17th, she speaks of the 50th anniversary of profession of another member of the community, and wonders if hers will come. "Sometimes I think it won't, but I have only the old cancer to judge on…the cancer reminds me of the Viet Cong – but not so immediately deadly!"

However, she is preparing to teach three courses, one of them on Saint Paul mostly for the young religious. But to her consternation, she has just learned that they come with

> 12 or more typed outlines of lectures by Mother Sullivan at Kenwood! But this course of mine was planned before we knew this – Woe is me! Kenwood gave no *description* of Scripture courses on the transcripts! Well, I also have Bonsirven,[54] which I don't always understand, but my students will!

---

[54] Joseph Bonsirven was author of many books on the New Testament. Here she probably means his *Saint Paul*, published in 1941.

Her last surviving letter to Margaret Byrne was written a few days later, on August 28.

> I am slowed up, Meg, and we have to admit it. Mother O'C.[55] should not have told you anything was "wronger" – things do sound worse than they are. The pain is bad ONLY AT TIMES – and I have every "soulagement" the Society can find to provide. The arm and hand were frightfully swollen from lack of circulation – now Dr. Missey had helped that very much, so I shall not be embarrassed by it in the classroom. The cause is very simple – pressure on the major vein or artery or something by the new lumps. I went to X-ray therapy for 3 weeks, every other day. Now I am off of that for a month to safeguard the surface skin. It is tender and just might break – and that would be hard to heal. Dr. Gafney takes the BEST of care of me and does not seem deeply concerned about the new recurrence, as I have survived the previous ones and like St. John the Beloved, in the old martyrology, have come out – not of boiling oil, of course, - stronger and healthier than before....
>
> The winds of change are blowing our way, however. We have discussed in community many things that other orders are changing – silence, for instance. It really is a psychological necessity, most of us feel – even the "young uns" – so I am hoping....The new habits are much in our thoughts and discussions. The models are not attractive in any sense – just commonplace and problematic in many ways. I dread what is ahead – but am not sure what IS ahead!

---

[55] Mary O'Callaghan, RSCJ, was born in Ft. Myers, Florida in 1915. She entered the Society in 1942 and was professed in 1950. She taught college classes in several colleges, and was on the faculty at Maryville at this time. Her fields were history and political science. She later traveled extensively internationally and was involved in many justice causes. She died in 2004.

UNEXPECTEDLY,
THE END

Louise had no idea how prophetic those words were. What lay ahead for the community was the change of habit in a few months, and many changes in liturgy, community life, and ways of thinking that she would have found very difficult, in spite of her forward thinking and openness. After her death, many who knew her reflected on how hard much of this change would have been for her, and how fortunate that she did not have to engage in it any further. What lay ahead for her personally was quite different. Early on the morning of October 18, word came that Reverend Mother Gertrude Bodkin had died at Kenwood. Louise was to join in death her former novice director. Here is the account of her death written the same day by someone in the Maryville community, probably Marion Bascom, RSCJ, for immediate circulation to other communities of the Saint Louis Vicariate.

> Maryville College
> 13550 Conway Road
> St. Louis, Mo. 63141

On the same day God has taken to Himself very suddenly two of the Society's greatest sufferers. It was a shock, though a long expected one, to hear of our holy and beloved Reverend Mother Bodkin's death this morning.

Mother Callan was not at breakfast to hear the details Reverend Mother Vicar gave us. She had wakened with the most extreme pain she had ever had in her long years of pain, but she dressed and groped her way from one end of the building to the other to find the Mistress of Health, Sister

Weitzel. [56] Of course she could not go to Mass though she hoped to attend the students' Mass at 9:00. (It will now be offered for her.) Later in the morning she was able to take a little breakfast and insisted that she felt better and must go to her Scripture class. It was an hour-and-a-half period, but the students found her as enthusiastic as ever. She put all she had into Joshua and the walls – and even sang a little. "It was such a happy class," one of her freshmen said. She came to the refectory at 12, but left at once. Sister Weitzel gave her some medication and left her to rest, and meanwhile phoned to try to get her into the hospital.

Shortly after lunch, Mother Alvena[57] was on her way to the chapel when she felt impelled to go to Mother Callan's room. Two aspirants who had cells near Mother Callan's were running down the corridor to get help. When Mother Alvena went in, Mother Callan was clutching her crucifix. "Yes," she said, "I am in great pain, but I mustn't complain." Mother Alvena saw that this was the end and called Reverend Mother. The few who were there[58] prayed by Mother Callan, but in about fifteen minutes, a little before one she stopped breathing. Father Luke was not able to reach her to anoint her till after her death.

Mother Callan had always said that she wanted to die in full armor. Everyone knows how very active she was. During the past few years she made the mall beautiful with her daily gardening, wrote a shorter edition of her life of Blessed Philippine, worked hard to get up-to-date materials for her

---

[56] Carolyn Weitzel, RSCJ, born 1910 in Frankfurt, Kentucky, entered the Society in 1941 and was professed in 1950. She taught science, served as infirmarian in several houses of the Saint Louis Vicariate, and died at Grand Coteau in 1974.

[57] Alvena Schraubstadter, RSCJ, was born in Saint Louis in 1901, entered the Society in 1924, and was professed in 1932. She served in several houses of the Saint Louis Vicariate/Province as teacher and mistress general. In 1966 she was assistant superior at Maryville. She died at Saint Charles in 1990. Though the custom in the Society was to call RSCJ by their family name, she was known by her first name because of the difficulty of her family name.

[58] The author was among them.

revision of *The Society of the Sacred Heart in North America,* helped to edit the Duchesne Guild Bulletin, took courses in Catechetics, went to Duchesne College, Omaha, last summer to hear Mother Sullivan's lectures on St. Paul, taught whenever she was allowed to, was always ready to substitute for a sick faculty member, had a vigorous apostolate in the parlor, gave talks on Blessed Philippine in many of our houses, and was always happy to conduct a visitor on a tour of St. Charles and Florissant, the last being Mother Coakley[59] two days ago.

To our very great regret, Mother Coakley had to cut short her visit to Maryville because of Reverend Mother Bodkin's sudden home-going. She left this morning without knowing that this was also Mother Callan's last day on earth.

Dr. George Gafney had tended her during her twelve years of suffering. When he was notified of her death he said, "She was one in a million."

Not only did Mother Callan teach until about an hour before she died, but in a sense she is still fulfilling her vow of education after death, for there will be a postmortem in the hope of helping other cancer victims.

Mother Callan was keenly interested in our group discussions about the renewal and took full part in them, always clearly pointing out and strongly upholding the spirit of the Society which she loved so much. She will find her place in the Society in heaven among the fervent, generous, courageous frontier souls, and Blessed Philippine will recognize in her a genuine and authentic daughter.

The requiem Mass will be at 9:30 on the feast of Mater Admirabilis.

---

[59] Margaret Mary Coakley, RSCJ (Mavi) was born in Cleveland in 1920, entered the Society in 1942, and was professed in 1950. She was mistress of novices at Kenwood 1959-1968 and provincial of the New York Province 1968-1974. She died in New York City in 2011. In 1966, she had come to Maryville to visit her former novices in the Doctrinal Formation Program.

The hours of the last class were 10:30-11:50 a.m. The topic of the class has passed into oral lore; there are several versions and the true one cannot be confirmed, since Maryville College's class schedules for that year have not survived. One news article gives it as "God and the World." Other sources say it was some kind of Scripture course, and the subject matter of the day lent itself to the story of Joshua and the walls of Jericho. All agree that she sang the song to her class with special energy and enthusiasm. Louise sang and dramatized the song in such a way that the students had no idea that she was mortally ill.

She came to the community refectory for lunch, but left immediately when the bell was rung for talking. One of the young religious who lived nearby knew that she was ill, because early in the morning while praying in her room, she was asked by Louise to come in and pray there – a most unusual request. When Louise left the refectory, the young religious followed her to her room to check on her. She found Louise lying on her bed in great pain. Louise knew that she was dying. She told her to take the first class relic of Philippine that she wore under her habit and keep it. She looked up at the sister with a look of radiance on her face and said: "The cancer didn't get me. It's my heart," and "I taught my class!" In a few minutes, Reverend Mother Mulqueen and other members of the community came into the room. Just a few minutes later, Louise stopped breathing. One of the priests from Saint Louis Priory rushed over to give her the Last Sacraments, but she was probably already dead. As can be imagined, the college students who had been in that late morning class were in absolute shock, as were even those in the community who knew how ill she had been and how much she had suffered.

The funeral Mass on October 20 was held in the Maryville College chapel. Her dear friend, Margaret Byrne, R.C., then superior at the Cenacle Retreat House in Warrenville, Illinois, was not able to attend because of important meetings of the Religious of the Cenacle that she was hosting. The presider was Father Luke Rigby, O.S.B., prior of nearby Saint Louis Priory. The homilist was her old friend Msgr. Curtin. An article in the Maryville newsletter *The Gong* (39:2; November 18, 1966) notes that he said that "the sometimes abstract Christian principles are defined and made concrete in the lives of such women as Mother Callan." She would have been happy that the Mass was celebrated with the new English liturgy in white vestments, in which "the spirit of joy is pervasive."

LES RELIGIEUSES DU SACRE-COEUR DE JESUS de la

Maison de........*Maryville*........................vous supplient très

humblement de recommander à DIEU au Saint Sacrifice de la

Messe et dans vos prières, l'âme de leur chère.....*Mère*............

........................*Louise Callan*........................

décédée le *18 octobre* 19.. âgée de *72* ans, *10* mois

10 jours, et de *Profession* *43* ans, *8* mois, *8* jours,

munie des Sacraments de notre Mère la Sainte Eglise.

Requiescat in pace

Louise Callan's death notice sent from Maryville to
other houses of the Society of the Sacred Heart

Gravestone, Calvary Cemetery, Saint Louis

76

Nun Kept Teaching To Last Hour of Life

Mother Louise Callan, R.C.S.J., noted historian, author, and professor of history and theology, continued teaching up to the last hour of her life Tuesday on the placid campus of Maryville College, despite a lingering pain from a fatal disease she knew she had for many years.

MOTHER LOUISE CALLAN

Unbeknown to the 25 freshman students in her theology course on "God and the World," the 72-year-old educator was wracked with severe pain at the time the class ended at 11:50 a.m.

LUNG CANCER

She died of lung cancer an hour later.

A member of the Order of the Sacred Heart, Mother Callan remained "chipper and lively" up to the last hour, said college officials. She had been plagued with the terminal disease for many years but she refused to discontinue teaching.

Mother Callan hid her suffering, said a college official, and many of her students were unaware of her fatal disease.

Her death ended 30 years of teaching history and theology at Maryville College.

She joined the faculty in 1934. After interrupting her career at Maryville to become principal of Villa Duchesne, the Academy of the Sacred Heart in St. Louis and at other schools in St. Charles, Cincinnati, and New Orleans, Mother Callan returned to Maryville in 1940.

WROTE TWO BOOKS

She held bachelor's, master's and doctor's degrees in history from St. Louis University. Author of two books on the work of the Sacred Heart Society, Mother Callan also was considered an outstanding historian.

Recently she was guest lecturer at the San Francisco College for Women.

She was a member of the Mississippi Valley, American, Missouri and American Catholic Historical Societies.

Born in Knoxville, Tenn., Mother Callan attended the College of the Sacred Heart in Cincinnati from 1911 to 1913.

ENTERED IN 1917

She entered the Sacred Heart Society at Albany, N.Y., in 1917 and took her vows seven years later.

A funeral Mass will be said at 9:30 a.m. Thursday at the Maryville College Chapel. Burial will be in Calvary Cemetery. She is survived by a niece.

Obituary notice in the *Saint Louis Globe-Democrat*, October 19, 1966

Mother Callan, History, Theology Professor, Noted Author, Musician, Dies at Maryville

An hour after teaching her 10:30 theology class on Tuesday, Oct. 18, Mother Louise Callan died. Although she had suffered intense pain for twelve years, she refused to let it interfere with her varied contributions to Maryville.

Mother Callan was born in Knoxville, Tennessee, in 1894, and entered the Society of the Sacred Heart at Kenwood in 1917. She received her B.A., M.A., and Ph.D. at St. Louis University, and served as mistress of studies at St. Charles, Villa Duchesne, the Rosary (New Orleans), and Clifton (Cincinnati).

At Maryville she was professor of American History, theology, and other subjects for 26 consecutive years, and was always ready to substitute, even in other fields, for teachers who were ill. Her wide range of interests and abilities prompted one faculty member to comment, "Everything she touched came to life."

Mother Callan kept up with the new developments in her fields; last summer she took a Scripture course at Duchesne College, Omaha. In addition to her regular teaching load, Mother Callan coached many girls who might not otherwise have been able to graduate.

She was the author of two volumes on the work of her order; The Society of the Sacred Heart in North America in 1937, and Philippine Duchesne, Frontier Missionary of the Sacred Heart in 1957. Last year this book appeared in abridged form.

A gifted musician, she directed the choir and Glee Club for many years, and was organist until the swelling of her hands forced her to stop. Mother Callan had volunteered to perform at the Faculty-Student Talent Show scheduled for Oct. 26. Proceeds will go to the Potawatomi Indians, one of her favorite charities.

As a member of the first group to take up residence at the new Maryville, she handled much of the work of moving, and later beautified the mall with her flower

(Continued on Page 4)

Teaching Was her profession, and Mother Callan evidently enjoyed it as she laughed with Nita Bell.

The Gong
Vol. XXXIX, No. 2   MARYVILLE COLLEGE, ST. LOUIS 63141   November 18, 1966

Maryville Participates Actively In Annual Catechetics Institute

"Ecumenism" is the theme of the Third Annual Catechetics Institute which will be held at Maryville Nov. 25 and 26.

Rev. Colman J. Barry, President of St. John's University, Collegeville, Minn., will open the Friday sessions with "The Ecumenical Direction of Vatican II." "The Future of Jewish-Christian Relations" will be the topic of Rabbi J. R. Rosenbloom of Temple Emmanuel in St. Louis. Dr. Warren Quanbeck of Luther Theological Seminary in St. Paul, Minn., will present "The Decree on Ecumenism: A Protestant Viewpoint."

On Saturday, Father Barry will begin the discussion of "Educating for Ecumenism." Rev. George Frein will take the Secondary level and

Maryville Art Gallery Features Ellen Wallach's Enamel Designs

Currently showing at the Maryville Art Gallery are fifty pieces of Ellen Wallach's enamels.

Mrs. Wallach's specialty is plaques depicting still lifes, portraits and abstracts. She has

Women's Press Club and of 2d Sullivan. Mrs. Wallach became interested in enameling because she "wanted to make some ashtrays for the living room."

Mrs. Wallach majored in Art

MOTHER CALLAN
(Continued from Page One)

garden.

The Requiem Mass was celebrated by Father Lake, O.S.B. at 9:30 a.m., Oct. 20, feast of Mater Admirabilis. In his homily, Msgr. James T. Curtin pointed out that the sometimes abstract Christian principles are refined and made concrete in the lives of such women as Mother Callan. The burial service followed the new English rite, in which the priest wears white vestments, and the "Dies Irae" is omitted, and the spirit of joy is pervasive.

Obituary notice in the Maryville *Gong*, October 18, 1966

MARYVILLE ALUMNAE NEWS
November, 1966   Page 1

4TH ANNUAL WORKSHOP

"Know Maryville Better" was the theme of the 4th Annual Workshop held Wednesday and Thursday, October 19 and 20. In addition to St. Louis chairmen and class agents, nine alumnae from other cities were present. (See picture.)

Presided over by Mrs. Henry J. Mohrman, the first session was opened with a prayer and welcome from Reverend Mother Mulqueen. Others who spoke included the Very Reverend Monsignor James T. Curtin, who enumerated the advantages of a small college; James Lord, president of the Student Council; and Sheila Daly, chairman of the Social Committee.

bers described various divisions of college work; Mother Patricia Barrett '35, Social Studies; Mr. Radko Jansky, the language lab; Dr. Edith Rich, biology; Miss Marian DeMeoli '42, mathematics and, in the absence of Mr. James Sala, Mr. Dennis Wachtel, the drama program.

Following the panel there was a meeting of the 1967 Fund workers, presided over by Mrs. Thomas Ballorna, general chairman. That evening the out-of-town alumnae were guests of the Executive Board at a dinner at Glen Echo Country Club.

Thursday morning started off with a student recruitment meet-

Memorial for Mother Callan

The Alumnae have added their expressions of grief to that of the students on hearing of Mother Callan's death. So many spoke of her gayety, her wonderful sense of humor, her deep scholarship, her intense devotion to the Sacred Heart. One former student spoke of her skill of "bringing the third dimension to her history classes." Letters have poured in from her countless friends, telling of the vivid role in their lives.

Some of Mother Callan's friends have proposed as a memorial to her the Music Department in the Fine Arts Building. Architects' preliminary plans are currently in the making and as we go to press several contributions have been received for the Callan Memorial.

FUND REPORT

Recently, alumnae, parents and friends of Maryville received the excellent report of the 1966 Fund

Mother Louise Callan, right and Mother Margaret Byrne RC, '14 photographed while visiting St. Charles several years ago.

Obituary notice in the Maryville Alumnae News, November, 1966

78

She Gave Life . . .

Mother Callan was a gardener. She gave life, nourished life, and cared for life. With her warm smile and sparkling eyes, she called forth the best in everyone, and rarely was disappointed. Mother Callan took joy in each aspect of life. She gloried in the history of the U.S., admired St. Paul, grew roses to beautify both the campus and the altar, and deeply loved blessed Philippine. The first place in her heart was held by Christ; her first concern was her students, yet she always had time to walk Buster.

Like Philippine, Mother Callan was a missionary. She spent her life giving life to others. She exemplified the teaching of Christ: "Let your light shine before men, that they may see your good works and give glory to your Father in heaven." Nothing is here for tears, nothing to mourn. We shall indeed miss Mother Callan, and we pray that we may be living monuments of her work.

THE GONG

Published Five Times a Year by
Maryville College
St. Louis 41; Mo.

All Catholic   All American

Editor   Catherine Barnett

Page Editors   J. Dunn, P. Jackimiec, M. Siemer. M Webster

Memorial reflection in the Maryville Alumnae News by Jan Dunn, then a Maryville student

ACKNOWLEDGEMENTS

With gratitude to:

First and foremost, Sister Margaret Byrne, RC, who saved Louise's letters over many years and made them available to Sharon Karam, RSCJ.

Collaboration between the author and Sharon Karam, RSCJ, with regard to memories, taped interviews, and study of the letters

Other sources:

Archives, Society of the Sacred Heart, United States-Canada Province
Registrar, Saint Louis University
Archives, Archdiocese of Saint Louis
Archives, Maryville University
Correspondence of Louise Callan with Margaret Byrne, RC, 1952-1966
Marion Bascom, "Five-Star Courage," *The Maryville Magazine* 42 (1967) 22-25
Louise Callan, RSCJ, "Mother Shaw: As I Knew Her," *The Maryville Magazine* 33 (May, 1958) 11-13

Interviews and written accounts:

Marion Bascom, RSCJ
Mary Blish, RSCJ
Margaret Byrne, RC
Jane Cannon
Mary Hagele, RSCJ
Marie Louise Martinez, RSCJ
Mary Gray McNally, RSCJ
Mary O'Callaghan, RSCJ
Margaret Seitz, RSCJ

Printed in the United States
By Bookmasters